"This revelatory, insightful, brutally honest book will actually help you! That's because Jamie Beaton has more experience than anyone, from his personal journey as a New Zealander to Harvard, Stanford, Oxford and Yale to his pioneering role as founder and CEO of Crimson Education, which has helped thousands of students crack the code of Ivy League admission. *ACCEPTED!* is the real deal—and fun to read to boot. Tiger Mother approved."

— *Amy Chua, John M. Duff, Jr. Professor of Law at Yale Law School.* New York Times *bestselling author of* Battle Hymn of the Tiger Mother *and* The Triple Package

"No one knows more about how to get into a top school than Jamie Beaton. This book is filled with actionable advice for improving your odds."

— *Adam Grant,* New York Times *bestselling author of* Think Again, Originals *and* Give and Take. *University of Pennsylvania Wharton School of Business top-rated professor for 7 straight years. Recognized as one of the world's 10 most influential management thinkers and Fortune's "40 under 40."*

"Higher education has always been exclusive, and in the last 5 years it has become even more so. Lean on Jamie and his experience to get into the best programs in the world."

— *Scott Galloway, NYU Stern Professor of Marketing and* New York Times *bestselling author of* The Four, Algebra of Happiness, and Digital IQ Index. *Elected to the World Economic Forum's "Global Leaders of Tomorrow," which recognizes 100 individuals under the age of 40 "whose accomplishments have had impact on a global level."*

"I spent 20 minutes with Jamie Beaton some years ago and jumped at the chance to invest in Crimson when it was a small company with huge success in New Zealand. He was not your typical 19-year-old. At an early age Jamie understood the importance of receiving the best education possible, and has tried to avail that to tens of thousands of students worldwide. Jamie is a force of nature who exudes passion, energy and intelligence during almost every hour of the day."

— *Julian Robertson, Founder of Tiger Management, and known as "The Wizard of Wall Street"*

"When I was growing up in country Australia, it was understood that you'd go into one of two careers: dairy or beef. The chance to attend a great university opened a world of opportunity for me. I hope this book will help bright, ambitious high school students from around the world shoot for the stars through higher education."

— *Kevin Rudd AC, Former Australian Prime Minister*

"If you spend any amount of time with Jamie Beaton, you will find him to be an exceptional and tireless individual. He figured his way from New Zealand to the best universities around the world. He systematized his insights and created Crimson Education to help aspiring students understand the college admission system. Now he brings those insights to *ACCEPTED!*, his very well-written and entertaining book. If you value entrance to a great university, this book is compulsory reading."

— *Alfred Lin, Partner, Sequoia Capital & #1 Venture Capitalists Globally in* Forbes Midas 2021

"Jamie is a true pioneer in the education landscape. Through his own experience studying at Harvard, Stanford, and Oxford, as well as the almost decade working alongside some of the world's most ambitious students, Jamie and the Crimson team have become the global leader in the University and College Admissions landscape. Jamie's innovative approach to working with students at the individual level, bringing together teams of industry specialists, has helped thousands achieve their dream admission result. Jamie is leading the way for others to follow."

— *Rt Hon Sir John Key: Former NZ Prime Minister*

"*ACCEPTED!* unveils Jamie's exceptional college admission strategies, which have helped numerous students worldwide go to their dream colleges. The book transforms our perspectives on college admissions and arms students with productive ways to envision their future life. It's a must-read for students as well as their parents!"

— *Tomohiro Hoshi, Head of School, Stanford Online High School, Lecturer Stanford University*

"For any student entering this brutal selection process this is a must read book, as it is for any parent who wants their child to receive the missive 'Accepted'. Congratulations, Jamie, on such a practical and pleasure-to-read book using your experiences of being a Rhodes, and a graduate of Harvard, Stanford and Oxford, sharing your brilliant and truly extraordinary journey with us.

— *Emeritus Professor David Buisson, University of Otago; Sloan Fellow MIT; Former Regional Chairman and Educational Counsellor for MIT undergraduate admissions*

"Jamie is a great source of inspiration, a visionary entrepreneur and above all, my life-long mentor and my dearest friend. I met Jamie at the end of high school when I desperately needed a scholarship to afford my college education, for which Jamie generously offered his guidance. Because of Jamie's support, I was fortunate to receive a full-ride scholarship from the Australian National University for my undergraduate study followed by master's degrees at Stanford and the Schwarzman Scholars Program at Tsinghua. The last eight years of growing Crimson with Jamie has been an extremely rewarding journey and a truly transformative experience – lots of which you'll be able to discover in this book!"

— *Fangzhou Jiang, Crimson Education Co-Founder, HURUN 30 Under 30*

"Don't just apply. . . stand out! In this fascinating book, Jamie Beaton shows how to position for admittance at the world's most famous universities. I wish I had this book when I was applying."

— *David Meerman Scott,* Wall Street Journal *bestselling author of 12 books including* The New Rules of Marketing and PR

"Jamie encourages students to maximize their potential and become inspirational leaders. Through his life, Jamie embodies the qualities that are most important in an educator - remaining a learner and embodying his teachings. His life's lessons are packed into this book, making it a must-read."

— *Ed Matsuda, Founder of Teach For Japan, The Most 100 Influential People in Japan* (Nikkei Business), *Crimson Education Japan - Country Manager*

"The first conversation I ever had with Jamie changed the course of my entire life. In the span of one hour, Jamie had turned my childhood dream of attending Harvard into a precise actionable trajectory that led me to gain admission to Harvard, Stanford, UPenn (Huntsman Program), Columbia, Brown, and Dartmouth, and more recently has led me to building a venture backed company. His book *ACCEPTED!* is an extremely punchy collection of the many kernels of wisdom Jamie has shared with me over this multi-year journey - an absolute must-read for anybody thinking about applying to competitive US/UK universities."

— Soumil Singh, Harvard University, also accepted to Stanford, University of Pennsylvania (Huntsman Program), Columbia, Brown, Dartmouth

"Jamie has taught a generation of students that the impossible is possible and now ACCEPTED! Is the playbook for that vision. This book will give you the insight of what it takes to aim for a target on the moon and hit the bullseye every time – accounting for the physics of moon-gravity and space junk that may come in the way. ACCEPTED! Is a rare look into the mind of a master strategist and how this mindset moulded an ambitious kid to a global leader."

— Rahul Sood, Wharton / UPenn CAS '20, Vagelos Program in Life Sciences and Management summa cum laude

"*ACCEPTED!* offers unparalleled, practical and 'can't-find-anywhere-else' insight on the ever shifting and increasingly competitive top college admissions landscape. I am evidence that Jamie's advice is golden. I never dreamed, when starting my applications, that I would have three Ivies and Stanford to choose from. There is no way I would be where I am today if not for what Jamie describes in this book. Read it and take his advice - it works!"

— Claudia F., Princeton University, also accepted to Stanford, the University of Pennsylvania and Dartmouth

"Jamie is exceptional — full of energy, ideas, and passion. He's the kind of person you go to when you have a wild, or rather, statistically improbable vision, and he possesses the conviction and skills to make it happen. At age 16, yearning for a community of intellectuals and change-makers, I aspired to go to one of the US's best universities. While I started knowing close to nothing about the nuances of the admissions process, I ended up receiving a Likely Letter from Stanford! Three years later, my sister also worked with Crimson and is now studying at Oxford. For our family, working with Crimson and Jamie has elevated our futures to new heights — enabling social mobility, world-class opportunities, and once-in-a-lifetime experiences."

— Rizina Y., Stanford University, also accepted to Princeton, Yale and Oxford

"Jamie has blown my wildest dreams out of proportion: I'm now living them. Following Jamie's advice, I was offered admission to my dream school - but also a full-merit scholarship that I wouldn't have dared to imagine myself capable of. Jamie will help you reimagine your possibilities. He's a visionary, but also a relentless pragmatist. There is no one more knowledgeable, passionate and hungry when it comes to college admissions."

— Jia D., Robertson Scholar at Duke University,
3 x VEX Robotics World Champion, also accepted
to Princeton, Columbia and Carnegie Mellon

"A thorough and thoroughly interesting guide to a world we think we know all about - wonderful!"

— Oscar E., University Of Pennsylvania, Wharton School of Business, also accepted to Yale and Cornell

ACCEPTED!

ACCEPTED!

Secrets to Gaining Admission to the World's Top Universities

Jamie Beaton
CEO, Crimson Education

JB JOSSEY-BASS™
A Wiley Brand

Jossey-Bass
A Wiley Imprint
111 River St., Hoboken, NJ 07030
www.josseybass.com

Library of Congress Cataloging-in-Publication Data is Available:

ISBN: 9781119833512 (paperback)
ISBN: 9781119833529 (epub)
ISBN: 9781119833536 (ePDF)

COVER DESIGN: PAUL MCCARTHY

SKY10031841_122321

Contents

Foreword

Former Prime Minister of New Zealand,
the Rt. Hon. Sir John Key

My mother learned the hard way the value of education.

She was 16 and living in Austria when the growing Nazi threat against Jews prompted her recently widowed mother to send her to safety in England. Although her mother survived the war, many of my extended family members died in concentration camps. People commonly talk of the "dark clouds" that were gathering over Europe in the prewar period. To my grandmother, mother, and the many family members I never had a chance to meet—and to millions of other people—the threat to their homes, livelihoods, friends, and families was very real. Those who could, fled.

My mother, Ruth, was an intelligent woman and she may well have had a good education in Austria had her life not been so brutally altered by World War II. Instead, she arrived in England speaking almost no English and with no way to further her formal education. In time, she married an Englishman and moved to New Zealand. I was the youngest of their three children. When my father died—I was at primary school—my mother once again set about rebuilding her life. And once again as an immigrant.

My mother instilled in me the need for a good education. Having herself lost the security she had depended on, first as a teenager, and then as a young wife and mother, she understood its value. This is a common thread in the story of many refugees and immigrants. A person and a family can lose almost everything—their home, their job, their friends, their citizenship—but they still retain their character, their education, and their skills. It's these that have allowed many people to start new lives.

Education is the ladder that can enable people to climb to heights otherwise thought unachievable. Education is also a currency that has value the world over. Like currencies, some education has more value than others.

This book focuses unashamedly on elite education. It's about how the cream of the world's universities select from some of the best and brightest students graduating from high schools around the world every year. The maths, as any of these bright students will tell you, are not on their side when they apply to Harvard, MIT, or Oxford. But in this book, Jamie Beaton generously shares his own first-hand and professional knowledge to help students tilt the table a bit more in their favor.

Students aspire to attend elite universities for a whole range of reasons, including the fact that a degree from one of them opens doors to employment at similarly elite global companies. These universities' selection processes, as you'll read in the following chapters, are so thorough and rigorous that employers of choice know much of the sorting task has been done for them.

It would be wrong to think anyone can simply game the university entrance system by trickery. That is not Jamie's argument here. Intelligence, hard work, and creativity remain the key requirements. But there are strategies, from course selection to choice of part-time jobs, that might increase a person's chances, and Jamie canvasses those in the following pages.

I am a graduate of the University of Canterbury in Christchurch, New Zealand, and had a great education there. It would be remiss of me to not remind ambitious young people that there is more than one pathway to success. Not getting into an elite overseas university might end one dream—but it needs to inspire another. In New Zealand, the worth of a person is not measured by which university they attended, if any. But it's true that what degree you complete, what grades you get, and where you studied will be something employers look at. Some of the global financial firms I worked in would hire graduates only from a select and prestigious group of universities. That didn't always sit well with me as a Kiwi who believes strongly in opportunity. But choosing graduates from selected schools was clearly a guaranteed way of tapping into a hugely impressive pool of highly talented people.

Countries like Singapore and South Korea, which, as nations, took deliberate steps to lift their economic game and to become more competitive, are in the same market for that talent. In the competitive market for skills, and with the increasing technological sophistication of even the most basic tasks, the desire by corporations and nations to feel confident that they are hiring people with the right answers is only getting stronger. Borders tend to melt away for those with the right education and skills. Their market is the world.

This book, based on the experience of Jamie and the thousands of students assisted and nurtured by Crimson Education, will help students and their families understand the selection systems of the world's top universities. It doesn't tell you what to do with your education once you have it—wherever you end up getting it. My message to students, like my mother's message to me, is to value whatever educational opportunities you have. Embrace challenges. Say yes to opportunity. Learn, and learn more. No knowledge is wasted.

If, like me, you have the opportunity in your career to give back to your community or your country, do so. The world is facing unprecedented environmental challenges and social strain is evident everywhere. Education has a private and a public benefit, and an elite education is likely to enhance the opportunity to build wealth and security for yourself and your family. But some of the greatest rewards and satisfactions in life come from using your education and achievements to lift up people you might never meet. You don't have to have an education to do that but, as in most things, it will certainly help.

To everyone reading this book, I wish you luck in your endeavors, and lots of caffeine at exam time.

Rt. Hon. Sir John Key

Introduction

When I was 15 I bumped into my school valedictorian on a train.

It was a chance meeting, but I took the opportunity to say hello, given the guy was my academic role model and being valedictorian—or as we called it dux—at King's was on my list of high school ambitions.

We stood and chatted as the train rocked and my backpack pulled on my shoulders and bumped into the back of another book-laden kid standing behind me.

I didn't say much, mostly listened, and if you asked me now exactly what this older kid said to me, I couldn't tell you.

But what I do know is that, when I got on that train I had my future all figured out: valedictorian, high school graduation, medicine at the University of Auckland. But by the time I got off, my entire plan had been shot to pieces and replaced with another, and all because this kid told me that he had gotten into Yale.

At this stage, of course, I had no idea what I was doing.

The best plan I could come up with was this: *more is definitely more.* Although other kids took three A Levels, I took ten. If my peers were making Top in New Zealand, I set my sights on making Top in the World (I made it for English Literature). If my older mate managed to get into

Yale applying to a handful of schools, I figured it was best to hedge my bets and increase my chances by pure volume, and so I applied to many of the world's top universities.

Of course, no one was more surprised than I was when I got into all of the greats I applied to: Harvard, Yale, Wharton (Hunstman), Cambridge, Yale-NUS, and more! I was just a skinny kid from the bottom of the world who narrowed the odds by going overboard.

So would I do it the same way again, given what I know now, given the people I've met and the places I've studied and the questions I've asked of scores of my mentors and peers at Harvard, Stanford, and Oxford?

The answer is yes and no.

We're all told time and time again that there is no secret formula of guaranteeing a spot at an Ivy or Stanford or MIT—and that is true, but only to a point, given like any highly sought-after goal, sooner or later you start to see a pattern. I started Crimson Education with my then-girlfriend at 17, on the floor of our respective parents' living rooms, and even then, I knew there was an art to what I'd done that went beyond any talent or element of luck that I'd unwittingly tapped into.

It is true that acceptance rates at Harvard, Stanford, and Princeton hover around the 4% mark—but 4% still get in. The trick is building an application that puts you in that 4%, and if you have the talent and the right strategy you can increase your chances significantly.

More may still be *more*, but these days tens of thousands of kids do that "more," so the secret lies not just in what you do, but the intricacies of detail behind it.

It's about the support you get, the mentors who engage, the time line you set, the strategy behind your application list, and knowing how to make every grade you achieve, and every written word on your application, count.

There's a reason the students we work with are up to four times more likely to get into an Ivy than the general applicant: they're bright and hard-working, but so are many thousands of kids out there with whom they're in direct competition.

As human beings we all like to think there is one secret solution to a frequently asked question such as "How do I get into Harvard?" But the truth is, that doesn't exist. What there *is*, however, is a set of secrets that align to increase your chances significantly. Think of it as getting on the train at one stop, ticking off a list of very specific stations, talking to the right people, shifting your balance so the ride is smooth and steady, and getting off at the other end with a whole new realization of what's possible.

So how will reading this book help you make your start?

ACCEPTED! is the embodiment of the best part of 25 years of high-intensity academics navigating the most difficult competitions required to get in and study at Harvard, Stanford, Yale Law School, the Rhodes Community, and more, as well as my experiences navigating the careers and education pathways for thousands of students across more than 20 countries.

Think of it as your own train ride from here to there, with "there" being admission to one of the best universities in the United States.

Ready to get started?

Jump on board!

Chapter 1

Signaling, the Hunger Games, and McHarvard

From the moment we are born, we are trained to compete for all things—for food, for partners, for a place to live, for our beliefs, and more. As our economy and education system has gone global, competition has only increased, and the returns to success have grown and grown as talented individuals can access much larger markets than ever before.

Certain countries like China and Singapore lean in on competition. From a young age, children in China prepare for the rigorous college entry exam—the Gaokao—which force-ranks a nation of learners and precisely determines which universities and even careers they can access.

In Singapore, children are streamed at each stage of learning, creating a gladiatorial system that at the highest levels in schools like Raffles Institution Singapore produce exceptional learners.

The biggest mistake made in the Western world, which I suspect will have more of an impact on why countries like China continue to grow in prominence at mindblowing speeds while countries like the US appear to trend sideways, is hiding from the competition that made these nations great in the first place. The classic story of the child at his weekend soccer game who may lack talent in that particular sport but is given a participation trophy for turning up because no one would want to shake his confidence seems kind and encouraging. But ultimately we have to ask if this approach leads to a false perception of reality, and more importantly, if it might dilute that child's ability to engage with the real world.

The real world is competitive. Colleges assess you on paper and look at your personality, extracurriculars, academics, and references to determine whether they will accept or reject you from their gates. Employers offer generous salaries to those individuals who pass this initial college admissions officer assessment—those who get in—effectively handing these students access to jobs and post-graduate degrees others will simply not have access to. Venture capitalists will invest millions behind a few select young people who have risen to the top of a competitive hierarchy and have identified trends in the market others haven't spotted.

Although it is nice to imagine a world in which the results of our youth do not meaningfully affect our future or an environment in which everyone is judged by their merits and on nothing else, this is terrible parenting advice for a young person. The reality is there is no launchpad that can propel you into a career of success, significance, and impact with the same consistency as a college degree from a top institution.

I've sent more than 1,000 students to the world's best universities, and like clockwork they land jobs at the types of institutions that offer life-changing opportunities: Blackstone, the world's largest private equity firm; Google DeepMind, the world's leading artificial intelligence lab; McKinsey, the world's most prestigious management consulting firm; Goldman Sachs, the world's most competitive investment bank. Despite the fact that these companies have massive resources, they can't go on a worldwide talent search for every single position. Rather, they inevitably gravitate to recruiting from the same pool of highly selective colleges. These colleges have already done a lot of the heavy lifting for them in assessing vast swathes of young people and deciding who can get in and who gets rejected. The colleges take the process even further: forcing their students to compete head-to-head, ranking them numerically with a grade point average that enables firms to easily assess who thrived and who struggled once they hit these bastions of competition and academic excellence.

As a young person, you can tell yourself that college doesn't matter or that high school has nothing to do with your career, but the reality is, in virtually all scenarios, the easiest and most effective path to success is getting into an elite college and making the most of that opportunity.

Many critics have asked why these elite colleges are important. Does Harvard have the best teachers? A lot of classes are taught by graduate students. Do the endless laboratories and resources really change the experience of the average student? I never set foot in one in my time there. Does Harvard have the best career advice? I never went into the on-campus career services—not a single time.

The answer to why these colleges are so important sits with a Nobel Prize–winning, human capital theorist, Gary Becker. Becker coined the phrase "signaling,"[1] which refers to the power of a student's education credentials to act as a signaling device to future employers or postgraduate admissions officers as to their superior innate abilities. In a busy world, no one has the time, money, or knowledge to be able to actually audit people's real ability. As a result, they rely on signals of quality in order to proxy real ability. The college degree is the ultimate signal of ability. How many times have we come across an Ivy League "genius" in a Hollywood movie like the Yale-educated data scientist played by Jonah Hill in *Moneyball*? Or the aspiring diplomat who happens to be a Rhodes Scholar (check out Charlize Theron in *Long Shot*)? Or as the ferocious corporate lawyer from Harvard Law School (Harvey Specter in *Suits)*? Nothing is a faster proxy for ability, skill, and academic firepower in mainstream media than your university education.

Now, let's get something straight. Is it true that the world's best 1,600 undergrads for a given year are all sitting in Harvard's seats? Absolutely not. Many of the world's best young people may not know that Harvard's financial aid policy means anyone who gains admissions can get enough funding to be able to attend. Many would never have considered applying. Many more may not have the opportunity to attend college because they have to financially support their family (which says reams about their character).

Regardless, the market is an efficient sorting mechanism that doesn't try to get everything right but get it approximately right. On average, will a Yale Law graduate be a fantastic lawyer? Probably, yes. On average, will an MIT artificial intelligence PhD be able to convince the public of the importance of some new data privacy laws over your average Joe? Probably, yes. On average, will a Stanford undergrad seem like the kind of person who could be the next unicorn founder in Silicon Valley? You bet (thanks Evan Spiegel![2]).

Signaling goes beyond just a college degree. There are signals on signals on signals. McKinsey can charge out their case teams at $1 million/week. Why? It might start with their nickname of "McHarvard" where they recruit seemingly endless numbers of Harvard graduates, Rhodes Scholars, and other talented young people from brand-name schools so they can market every case team as being full of "whiz kids." A million/week for primarily 22- to 26-year-olds with limited work experience on your most pressing business issues? It sounds like a scam. But these young people went to a top college. Okay, then that makes sense.

Now let's think about Silicon Valley. My cofounders at Crimson have been able to raise more than $US60 million before our 25th birthdays. This is our first business. We have no track record. Prior to going to Harvard, I really genuinely thought entrepreneurship was what you said you would do if you found yourself unemployed. This is rare but it is by no means a major exception. The most popular schools of unicorn founders (companies valued above $US1 billion) in the US were Stanford, Harvard, UC Berkeley, MIT, and the University of Pennsylvania (Wharton School of Business).[3] As a venture capitalist writing big checks with other people's money, being able to assure your investors that your entrepreneur is "investable" (a term I first heard from GGV investor Hans Tung, that is, they have impressive academic credentials that give a good clue that the person is of substance and likely to succeed) captures the power of signaling perfectly.

Fast-forward to a corporate boardroom for an executive appointment at a major technology company. A partner from one of our venture capital firms said to me that they only consider an executive at this level for a strategy role if they have been trained by one of the greats: Bain, McKinsey, or Boston Consulting Group. Hold on? If these management consulting firms hire based on the signal of a college degree and now it is indeed those firms that are acting as the signal for executive hires—what does that mean?

The answer is obvious. Your college degree is incredibly important. It sets up a reputational snowball that will affect every facet of your working life. It may even affect your dating life!

When I first wrote about this at the age of 16 in our student newspaper at King's College, my wonderful English teacher told me to shelf the article because it was "too depressing." Why? I'd wondered to myself.

As long as you as a young person or a parent go into education with eyes wide open, understanding the Herculean high-stakes competition in front of you and how to beat it, knowing this is one of the most impactful things you can do for your motivation, then it is not depressing but just a situation you know you need to negotiate.

Once negotiated, the rewards are limitless and all the effort expended are not just worth it but life changing in more ways than you can imagine. So let's dive into the nitty gritties starting with my first piece of strategy advice on class spamming—the ultimate case of when more means more.

Chapter 2

Class Spam
Deadly and Effective

Many students spend hours and hours trawling online forums, asking friends, mentors, and alumni of top universities: what activities do I do to get into a top university?

The best answer to this question is comically simple but brutally effective.

As an 18-year-old, I applied to Harvard, Yale, Princeton, Stanford, Wharton, and Cambridge and gained admission to all of them. I beat students who were smarter than me, had Mathematics Olympiad Medals, were head students of their school, and had a wide variety of other achievements. What was my strategy?

Take the maximum possible academic subject load and do more than any other student around you.

But what exactly does this mean? At my school, King's College, a well-to-do private boarding school where I was studying on a scholarship, the typical student would take three to four A Levels (in the Cambridge curriculum).[1] But I did 10.

Taking a subject load that was 2.5 times the median student and more subjects than anyone else in my school's history showed that on one very important dimension—academic capacity and work ethic—I was demonstrably able to beat everyone else. I didn't take on all that extra work simply to lay claim to this record, it wasn't about "winning" for the sake of winning. I simply had my sights set on top US or UK university admission, and at the time, doing more sounded like the best way to increase my chances of getting in. Which ultimately it did, and for other students still does. One of my students in Shanghai this year just finished his 17th AP subject. (Update: he was accepted into Harvard in the 2021 admission cycle.)

So why does this work? Many universities like Stanford seek to test intellectual vitality.[2] Broadly, this means they want to know that you are interested in a wide variety of fields, are open to discovering new subject areas, and that you pursue academic initiatives outside of school that you weren't forced to take in the classroom.

Naturally, you could try and show Stanford that you like business and economics by listing a bunch of books that you have read (I like *AI Superpowers*[3] and *Freakonomics*[4] myself), but what is the most efficient way to show you mean business? Take an accredited subject in that field. It could be AP Microeconomics, AP Macroeconomics. It could be A-Level Economics or A-Level Business Studies. This is the most efficient way to communicate to the university that you are passionate about the subject, trained in the subject, and cared enough to go through the ordeal of sitting a whole additional exam in the subject.

In high school, I took extra subjects in Further Mathematics, Mathematics, Biology, Chemistry, Physics, Thinking Skills,

French, English Literature, Business Studies, and Economics. I took the science subjects, maths, and English in school (these subjects were referred to inappropriately as the "Asian 5" for being the most serious subjects) and then proceeded to take subjects such as Economics *outside* of school ("self-studied").

Self-study, as I define it, refers to taking a subject outside of your traditional school. You could self-teach it, you could enroll in a part-time course offering like Crimson's online high school, Crimson Global Academy, or you could hire a tutor for it. The point is, you aren't taking it as a student in your traditional school. You're choosing to do extra.

Why is this strategy so effective? A university is trying to guess at who the most competent students are. When they read about your extracurriculars they may ask themselves, what does this mean? How legitimate is this organization? Did this really take much time? How passionate is this student? The main issue with extracurriculars and most other activities is there are very few universal standards that can clearly translate to an admissions officer exactly what you've done. (Not that extracurriculars are not *crucially* important to the college admissions process— they are, and we will get to that later. But they are viewed alongside your academic record, which you have to nail first.) When an admissions officer sees you've written an independent report on business in Japan, they will be intrigued but they will have limited comparability when they evaluate you against other students—when they place you head-to-head.

That is why this subject strategy is important. If you have completed 20 AP classes—and your best competitors have 17 or 15 all with similar grades, the university needs to actively find a reason to admit the other students over you. You will be the default pick because on the most clearly understood qualification you are ahead, and so on a risk-adjusted basis, your typical university will choose you.

If your school doesn't use the AP courses (in recent years a number of top US private schools have shifted away from the AP curriculum in favor of honors courses at the advanced placement level)[5], then take extra credits at the honors and advanced levels—and ideally at a higher volume than your friends.

Of course, if you ask your teachers, your counselors and even most university admissions officers who are still employed by a university, they will tell you to calm down. You don't need to take so many subjects! That is totally unnecessary! Universities don't want to see kids spending all their time on exams!

But the reality is, after sending thousands of students to the world's best universities and analyzing more than a million college admissions data points, the information is clear. The more subjects you take and the more standard deviations above the typical caseload of your school, the more likely you are to get into a top college. If I had to go back in time and compete in high school to get into Harvard as a 13-year-old now, I would simply start early, take more subjects, and still make my intensive academic load a primary competitive advantage in my application. Bottom line, every piece of data shows that there is a direct correlation between effort and acceptance to these top schools—and the higher the rank of the school the more effort you need to put in (see Figure 2.1).

The same argument applies to top schools in the UK such as Oxford and Cambridge, or Oxbridge as they are collectively called (see Figure 2.2).

This brings me to the concept of "competency learning," which is integral to your success. The system of modern schooling was built during the industrial revolution to

Figure 2.1

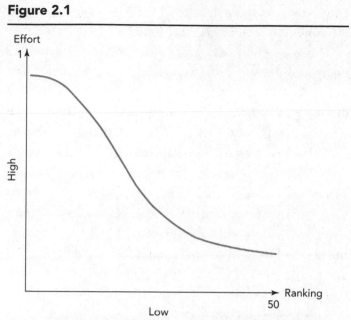

The amount of effort required to enter top 10 US universities is substantially higher than the effort required to enter top 30–50 schools. Beyond the top 50, the relationship between ranking and required effort quickly plateaus.

Figure 2.2

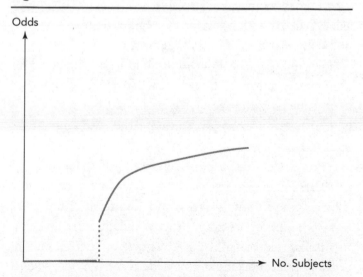

Students at Oxbridge universities are 0.70x as likely as students at UK universities in general to have taken three A-Level subjects, but 4.14x as likely to have taken four A-Level subjects, and a whopping 8.74x as likely to have taken five-plus subjects.

efficiently push through large volumes of students to learn the same core skills in the same time frame.

This is generally okay for a typical student. But you are not typical. You are trying to get into one of the world's best universities. By necessity, you have to beat the curve. One of the best ways to do this is to throw the concept of time and year levels out the window. An international diploma called the International Baccalaureate (IB)[6] is quite popular with students and illustrates this point well. For example, in most IB schools, you take a fairly random curriculum up until the last three years. In the better schools, in your third last year (Grade 10 in the US) you might take the International General Certificate of Secondary Education (IGCSE) and then in Year 11 and 12 (your junior and senior years), you sit the IB Diploma.

This means you don't actually get any formal qualifications until the last three years of high school, and you don't even get your final IB exam results until *after* high school finishes, and after you've applied to college. The truth is, most students can actually handle much of the content for subjects like the AP, or honors, far earlier than they are traditionally encouraged to take them.

Take my Crimson Education alumni Tristan Pang, for example. He finished the equivalent of his high school–level math courses at the age of 13. He's smart but perhaps his best advantage was he just started earlier and ignored the guidelines as to what age you can do what.

Taking 20 APs sounds difficult, but if you space that over five years rather than two years, you can achieve many more subjects, stagger out the stress and the pressure, and make time for re-sits, more exam sittings, and, importantly, fun.

All that said, as far as the strategy goes, there is one incredibly important thing you need to remember. *Quality comes first, then quantity.*

I took 10 A Levels, but if I would have completed them all with Bs and Cs, that would have been terrible. With AP subjects, anything below a 4 is not acceptable. You first need to make sure you can nail a given subject. Once you have achieved 4/5 in the AP, or a similar standing in honors classes, then you can take additional subjects. I'd rather have 10 AP courses with top grades than 20 with bad. This is because you need to show mastery in the subjects you take.

Although it is possible you are passionate about a subject you are bad at, the bottom line is, top universities have a lot of students to choose from. They don't need to choose you if you are passionate about economics but bad at it. They will alternatively pick the student who is passionate about economics *and* good at it. So the obvious piece of advice here is to try as hard as you can to get good grades in all the exams you take.

The exception to the quality first then quantity rule is the law of diminishing returns. There is a big difference between getting a 5 in AP BC Calculus and getting 100% and every question right. In this case, there is literally no university admissions benefit at all and getting a single point right above and beyond the threshold required to get a 5 in the AP. It would actually be extremely difficult to get the whole exam right. As a result, you should almost never be studying so much that you are seriously aiming for 100%. The effort required to go from 95% to 100% in most exams is more effort than the effort required to go from 0 to 90%. This effort is not worth it. *Use it to take more subjects!*

Make sure all your subjects are ideally in a single curriculum or at most two. For example, doing IB and then some A Levels and then AP spreads your work too thinly and makes you look relatively worse. Going super hard on a given curriculum is going to result in a more re-markable comparison for top universities. This means you need to choose your high school and your curriculum carefully so you don't find yourself switching schools in the middle.

Finally, and somewhat cheekily, if possible, do not tell all your classmates about all your additional subjects (admittedly this is difficult in some schools where APs/honors classes are populated by the same group of ambitious students). The whole point of this strategy is to take way more subjects than anyone else applying for the same universities.

In high school, I discussed my strategy with my closest friend and it resulted in that friend taking almost double the subjects they normally would. You don't want to create competition inflation by broadcasting publicly you are taking so many extra subjects, and then your classmates respond by taking more themselves. This effectively cancels out the benefit of your additional work as you no longer shine as bright relative to them. With college admissions, the less you can do to panic your classmates into taking more subjects, more exams, and more activities the better—that only creates more work for you! (I want to add here, however, that some of the best friends I have made are the ones who have challenged me to do better. So on that note, if you have a friend who stands out above the crowd, think about how you can use their example as inspiration for reaching your own potential.)

My parting words on this strategy: if you start early, stagger your subjects over many years, enabling you to resit and remove pressure and, of course, take subjects you are genuinely interested in, you can dramatically improve your odds of getting into an elite school. This strategy was the most important driver for my getting into Harvard,

Yale, Princeton, Stanford, and Wharton, and all the content wasn't for nothing. The broad knowledge of science and humanities has continued to pay dividends for me on Wall Street, building my company, succeeding in my undergraduate and graduate studies, and making like-minded friends in the process.

Chapter 3

Early Decision and the Dating Game

When it comes to love, you want to find the one person you care for so dearly, and connect with so completely, that you're ready to commit your entire life to that person. You want to be honorable, faithful, and sincere. With colleges, you need to be that kind of lover—just a lot more fickle.

US universities have invented a fairly complicated system of early admissions in order to try and unpack whether or not you actually like them. One of Crimson's partners is *US News & World Report,*[1] the leading global ranking organization for US universities. An important criteria to the all-important rankings for US universities is the "yield rate," which is the percentage of students who accept an offer from that university. Harvard, for example, has a yield rate that hovers about 81%. This means that for every 100 offers Harvard gives to students around the world, 81 offers are actually accepted. This is a crucial statistic to study alongside acceptance rates when researching a university because it shows how desirable the school actually is to the competitive kids who have been able to get in. (See Chapter 15 for more explanation!)

If you're a university like Brown, you are in a very complicated situation. You are a prestigious Ivy League school so life should be easy—but it's not. Brown wants to reject all unqualified students who are not sufficiently talented in the eyes of their admissions office to attend the school. At the same time, they need to admit students who are good enough to go to their school. The problem is, many of these qualified students have options. Almost all of these students would rather go to Harvard, Yale, Princeton, Stanford, MIT, or Columbia over Brown. This means that when Brown admits a student, they can't actually be sure that student is going to turn up come the fall.

Every time they admit a student who turns them down it is reflected in their ranking because this rejection diminishes their yield rate. As a result, Brown doesn't actually want to admit all qualified applicants who are strong enough to get in. Rather, they want to admit students who are qualified enough to get in but also who are willing to *commit* to their school.

This means that if they come across a truly exceptional Harvard-quality student who they are confident is going to get into one of the most competitive universities ranked higher than them, they may actually consider putting them on a waitlist rather than accepting them because they think it is highly unlikely the student would actually end up coming. It seems bizarre: Brown would decline a Harvard-quality student. Yet, the most sophisticated universities know this as fact.

This dynamic has led to the creation of the early decision application process. Prospective applicants can choose to apply early decision to a university (and with the Ivies you can only choose one), which means applying on roughly November 1 of your application year. If you apply early decision and you are accepted, you've committed to go to that university. This is a hard guarantee. No more applications in the regular round. That's it. If they accept you, you are done.

Unsurprisingly, early decision application processes have become widespread across top universities because they enable the university to guarantee a pool of applicants who will definitely attend their school. Admitting a student from the early decision pool gives a university a close-to 100% yield rate over this pool of applicants.

Now—guess which Ivy League universities *don't* offer early decision processes? Harvard, Yale, and Princeton. They will say all kinds of things—like they want to give talented students options—but in reality, they don't offer the early decision process because they don't need to. They know that generally speaking, when they admit a student, the student will be so over the moon they've been admitted that they will usually accept with a very high probability. Princeton may lose some students to Harvard, but generally speaking, at this highest of tiers, these universities back themselves as the premium choice for most people applying. Harvard, Yale, and Princeton offer early action instead, which is a way for candidates to apply earlier than the regular round (similarly about November 1 of your last high school year) but you are not forced to go to the school and you can apply to other universities in the regular round.

This is the option I chose back in November 2012. I applied and was accepted early to Harvard, then applied in the regular round to many more schools such as Yale,

Princeton, Stanford, and others. Ultimately, after doing the work to apply to many other universities and getting in, I still chose Harvard. They were right in offering early action, because in the end, it was hard to say no to Harvard.

The other Ivy League schools—the University of Pennsylvania, Columbia, Brown, Cornell, and Dartmouth—all offer early decision processes. These are great schools, of course, but given it's highly likely the students applying to their school are also applying to Harvard, Yale, or Princeton (HYP), they want to know that in choosing to applying to them early, you are committed—just like that lover I spoke about earlier—and that they won't lose you to HYP or Stanford or MIT later down the regular decision line.

Some schools have become even more sophisticated in their early application process. My favorite example is the University of Chicago. Beyond their hilarious and complicated essays (in my application year, one question was "So where is Waldo, really?" requiring a 500-word response), they have optimized their early application process and in doing so helped boost their ranking significantly. As I write this, University of Chicago is ranked sixth in North America for best undergraduate universities, ahead of many Ivy League schools.

University of Chicago[2] offers several admissions rounds:

1. Early action (due November 2)
2. Early decision I (due November 2)
3. Early decision II (due January 4)
4. Regular decision (due January 4)

As of October 2020, UChicago has won 100 Nobel Prizes.[3] A full 33 of these are Nobel Prizes for economics. Even my favorite Nobel Laureate, Gary Becker, who invented signaling, went there. It is no surprise that they have perfected the game theory and signaling of college admissions.

Both early decision rounds I and II are binding so if you apply in these rounds you are committing to go. Can you guess why UChicago does this? UChicago offers a binding and a nonbinding admissions option at each stage so they can filter you by level of seriousness. Twice!

If you are applying early action to UChicago, they know you are pretty organized and relatively interested in UChicago, but they also know that you're not interested enough to commit. This almost certainly means you like another early round university better or have higher hopes in the regular round. As a result, applying early action to UChicago is a death sentence. The admissions rate applying early action to UChicago is substantially lower than the early decision I rate.

The fun continues in the regular round. Most schools offer a purely regular admissions round where you can apply, get an offer, and then choose whether you want to go. But not the smart economists at UChicago. They want information from you—how much do you *really* like them? In the regular round, if you apply early decision II you have a dramatically higher admissions shot than applying regular decision. I recently saw a student with 15+ AP 5s get declined from UChicago regular decision. He was incredibly qualified, a very strong applicant, and UChicago knows that. But why is he not applying early decision II? Because he thinks he can do better and doesn't want to commit to UChicago. UChicago, by designing this system, knows this as well and denies that highly qualified applicant, keeping their high yield rate intact.

UChicago uses their complicated admissions options to filter the surges of qualified applicants into two buckets: qualified applicants who are prepared to declare their love to UChicago and want to commit, and qualified applicants who are not ready to sign on the dotted line. They decline the flighty prospective lovers in droves and focus on those who are ready to show their commitment.

Talk is cheap and action means everything, but UChicago hasn't finished having fun with you just yet. They even want to see whether you will profess your love for them in writing and test just how cheap your talk is. UChicago has one of the most complicated admissions essays of any of the major US universities. They ask two questions:

1. How does the University of Chicago, as you know it now, satisfy your desire for a particular kind of learning, community, and future? Please address with some specificity your own wishes and how they relate to UChicago.

    They then require you to answer a second question. In the 2020–2021 admissions cycle, they ask you to choose at least one from the following essay choices:

2. a. Who does Sally sell her seashells to? How much wood can a woodchuck really chuck if a woodchuck could chuck wood? Pick a favorite tongue twister (either originally in English or translated from another language) and consider a resolution to its conundrum using the method of your choice: math, philosophy, linguistics . . . it's all up to you (or your woodchuck).

    b. What can actually be divided by zero?

    c. The seven liberal arts in antiquity consisted of the Quadrivium—astronomy, mathematics, geometry, and music—and the Trivium—rhetoric, grammar, and logic. Describe your own take on the Quadrivium or the Trivium. What do you think is essential for everyone to know?

    d. Subway maps, evolutionary trees, Lewis diagrams. Each of these schematics tells the relationships and stories of their component parts. Reimagine a map, diagram, or chart. If your work is largely or exclusively visual, please include a cartographer's key of at least 300 words to help us best understand your creation.

e. "Do you feel lucky? Well, do ya, punk?"—Eleanor Roosevelt. Misattribute a famous quote and explore the implications of doing so.

f. Engineer George de Mestral got frustrated with burrs stuck to his dog's fur and applied the same mechanic to create Velcro. Scientist Percy Lebaron Spencer found a melted chocolate bar in his magnetron lab and discovered microwave cooking. Dye-works owner Jean Baptiste Jolly found his tablecloth clean after a kerosene lamp was knocked over on it, consequently shaping the future of dry cleaning. Describe a creative or interesting solution, and then find the problem that it solves.

g. In the spirit of adventurous inquiry (and with the encouragement of one of our current students!) choose one of our past prompts (or create a question of your own). Be original, creative, thought provoking. Draw on your best qualities as a writer, thinker, visionary, social critic, sage, citizen of the world, or future citizen of the University of Chicago; take a little risk, and have fun!

Many US universities offer supplementary essays as a way of enabling applicants to express why they like the university. The real reason they want to give you extra essay questions relates to the concept of the early decision round. They want you to "reveal your preferences" and show how seriously committed you are to the school.

If you write an essay to a college like Columbia about why you want to go to that school and you offer generic diatribes about New York, their core curriculum and the need for broad exploration, diverse classmates and other generic answers, they know you really haven't researched the school in detail. The really winning supplementary essays (which take a long time to write!) have to be so specific that what you can say literally ONLY apply to the single college you are applying to.

Some application essays are quite generic from school to school. They might ask you to describe the community you are from, for example. Unsurprisingly, high schoolers in the frenetic rush to apply to college, who have procrastinated writing application essays, try to copy/paste answers from school to school. This is the death cross! A university that can detect you are just answering with generic responses, and not customized to their university, knows that you are just spraying across multiple universities hoping one admits you. And let's be honest—they are usually right. For every one student I meet who genuinely loves a certain single university and is head over heels in love with it for a set of specific reasons, I would literally meet more than one hundred students who choose based on rankings a set of prestigious schools (and my previous arguments justify this as being rightfully so, in not all, but many cases).

University of Chicago wants to handbrake the spray-and-pray, copy/paste application essay strategy and force you to use your time to answer their truly cryptic prompts. I consider myself reasonably sharp holding several degrees in applied mathematics and have written academically in law school and doctoral programs but answering a question such as "what can actually be divided by zero" is very difficult. It is difficult by design. UChicago wants to force you to do a bunch of extra work that will only be relevant to their school. They do this so that they can shake off all the candidates who aren't that committed and who can't be bothered to write their complicated essays.

Between testing your willingness to "talk" through the difficult supplementary essays to testing your "action" through their binding admissions process, UChicago has mastered the game theory of admissions for a school that is highly prestigious but not considered in the upper echelons of competitive colleges. In doing so, they have shot up the rankings in recent years, artfully manipulating their yield rates and reading through the masses of college admits to find the kids who are really willing to commit. Good on them—but I hope for your sake that the other colleges don't copy UChicago!

You'll notice that nowhere does UChicago publish the specific acceptance rates by the stream of binding versus nonbinding. They never will (unless they are forced to under massive public pressure). This is intentional because they don't want you to actually think about this too deeply and try and game their attempt to game you. On their Class of 2024 admissions page[4] for example, they list only that they accepted 2,511 students, enrolled 1,848 students, and had 34,372 applicants. This translates to a mind-blowing yield rate of 73.6%. This is *only* beaten by Harvard and Stanford with 81–82% yield rates. UChicago beats MIT, Princeton, Yale, UPenn, and Dartmouth on yield rate. Arguably, all of these other colleges are usually more desirable for applicants than UChicago, but through designing an application process that ruthlessly filters kids, they have been able to game their yield rate and shoot above their peer schools landing at an enviable *US News* ranking.[5]

I hope UChicago doesn't get too angry at me for revealing their strategy, but power to the student I say!

UChicago aside, what are the key learnings for you?

First, almost every student reading this should apply early decision. We all want to have a shot at applying to Harvard and Stanford, but I can tell you with absolute certainty that every year when I look at most applicants, they really have no realistic shot and shouldn't waste their breath applying. Giving up an early decision option to have a shot at applying early action to Harvard, Stanford, Yale, Princeton, or MIT is usually crazy. Most applicants cannot get into this tier of school but try anyway, and in doing so, end up getting to a far worse eventual university than the school they could have been admitted to if they had committed early decision.

If you miss the early decision opportunity, and then have to apply in the regular round, you will find yourself swimming in an ocean of talented kids who are all bombing out applications to eight-plus schools each. So unless you have a very strong profile, you'll be submerged by the competition.

Generally in life you should be optimistic, but when it comes to university early decision time, you need to swallow your pride and be pragmatic. Wipe your tears if your dream school is Harvard but your SAT score is 1490. It probably isn't happening. That is okay. Don't let your ego stop you from not committing early to one of the many brilliant choices that require a binding commitment and locking in your offer. This is an important critical decision. Make sure you ask an expert which college you can realistically get into in the early round.

Second, be a flighty lover and preach your love to everyone (bad advice in life but good for college admissions!). What am I talking about? In your supplementary essays you need to hit each school with crafted essays that highlight exactly why you love their school with super-specific examples that only apply to their university and no other. This makes it more credible that you actually sincerely love their university beyond all others, and that's why they are more likely to admit you, assuming that you will, in turn, take their hand when they offer it.

Let me give you an example. If you apply to Harvard, the crowd favorite, you can tell them that you love them because they are a high-ranking, prestigious university. You can tell them they have myriad classes to choose from, offer a wonderful liberal arts education and many extracurriculars like debating and Model UN that extend your passions. You can tell them you want to take advantage of unique research opportunities and meet inspiring, diverse classmates.

But that would be a terrible essay.

Go back and read that last paragraph. Scratch out Harvard and you could say the same thing about Yale or Princeton or any other reasonable university. That is the test you have to do. If a single sentence of your supplementary essay can apply to another university, try again—it probably isn't specific enough. I've sent more than 50 students to Harvard alone and any opportunity we have to showcase their specific interests in Harvard, we focus on communicating what Harvard, as a magnificent institution of learning, offers uniquely as Harvard.

Let's say you like economics, business, and finance (a good portion of applicants). What could you talk about when applying to Harvard?

You could mention Harvard Student Agencies, the world's largest student-run business organization that lets you as a freshman manage retail stores and get practical hands-on management experience.

You could talk about the unique Statistics with Quantitative Finance track. This was introduced in the last decade as the interest in students going into quantitative trading has grown enormously. Very few other universities offer anything like this.

It might be nice to mention the legendary Professor Blitzstein who teaches the wildly popular Statistics 110 who makes even the most abstract statistics concept fun and understandable with his thought experiments.

You might want to mention the Harvard i-Lab. This is an entrepreneurial launchpad that lets students launch their own company, find mentors, gives them an office space to work from, and opportunities to meet investors. It is a relatively well developed incubator compared to most colleges.

You could mention popular student-run finance extracurricular organizations such as Black Diamond Capital, a student-run hedge fund that lets you trade the market with your "partners" or Harvard Financial Analyst Club (HFAC), which will train you up on how to value a stock in no time.

You could even mention the unique full-course exchange program with MIT that lets you take literally any class from the MIT catalog giving you access to MIT Sloan School of Management's fantastic finance and accounting coursework, while enjoying the benefits of Harvard's amazing liberal arts foundations.

You could talk about Professor Edward Glaeser's legendary Economics 1011a, one of Harvard's hardest undergraduate classes, with alumni like Steve Ballmer and Bill Gates. This gives you a rigorous training on Lagrangian optimization and economic modeling, which will be useful for any aspiring econ PhD students.

The list goes on. I expect this level of detail for any supplementary essay you write for any school you are serious about. This is the standard I hold my Crimson students to and support them to reach.

Do all those love letters (supplementary essays) sound a little bit difficult? Remember for the price of true, binding early commitment, UChicago might even accept you . . . and put you out of your misery!

Chapter 4

Morpheus Wins

"Show Me The Future!"

If you go to most college admissions offices in the US, attend an admissions tour, and ask the people who work there if there is a strategy to what major you should apply to on your Common Application, they will stare at you, just a little offended, and tell you with a poker face as if no other answer will do justice to your question: "You should apply for what you love!"

Wrong.

Pay close attention because this is a relatively unsettling but crucial strategy to understand and master.

When you apply to most US universities, you have to declare your academic interests or potential majors. A major is the focus area for your degree. Some universities may call this a different thing. Harvard calls their majors *concentrations,* for example. In essence, the university wants to know what you actually intend to study when you turn up on campus.

If you look at Stanford, the most popular major of choice is computer science.[1] It makes perfect sense. Computer scientists from Stanford can go on and earn $US100 thousand+ at major technology companies and live comfortably knowing they have a wide spectrum of choices. They can go and raise money from venture capitalists who trust that Stanford gave them some coding skills and recruiting networks they need to be successful. Computer science is a versatile skill that builds mathematical reasoning, data analysis skills, creativity, and logic in spades. It is a fantastic but difficult major. Among Crimson alumni, it is the second most popular area for coursework.

If you look at Harvard, the most popular major of choice is economics.[2] It makes perfect sense. Economists from Harvard go on to work on Wall Street in large numbers. They intern at Goldman Sachs, Morgan Stanley, JP Morgan, some may go onto legendary private equity firms like Blackstone or venture capital firms like Tiger Global. Economics can be applied to business and finance but the training is broadly applicable to almost anything from political campaigns to law school. It is hard to go wrong. Amongst Crimson alumni, it is the most popular area for coursework. I have a soft spot for economics because it was my main area of study at Harvard.

Can you guess what is a terrible major to apply for when you apply to Stanford or Harvard?

The worst major to apply for at Stanford? The prize goes to computer science!

The worst major to apply for at Harvard? The prize goes to economics!

Economics at Harvard is generally the most competitive major to apply to. The admissions office knows that everyone who says economics will generally go on to study it and many more who declare other majors will likely switch to economics anyways. As a result, they are desperate to find people with sincere academic interests in other areas to create a "diverse class." They don't want four aspiring Wall Street bankers sitting around Cabot dining hall discussing summer internships. They prefer a folklore and mythology major who can educate a physics major about topics that could also help a social studies major develop ideas for their thesis over dinner. If you apply for the most common, popular majors at a university you immediately make landing your offer substantially more difficult. You become a dime-a-dozen commodity.

When you apply to a US college, they generally accept you into the undergraduate program. You can switch to any major you like (with some exceptions) after you are admitted (you don't have to declare your major until the end of your second or sophomore year). Harvard never looks back on your application and checks what academic interests you declared and then scolds you for studying something totally different once you get to college. They actively encourage "intellectual discovery" in the first 18 months as you find your major/concentration of choice.

So what game do you need to play here?

You want to express academic interests that give you the highest possible chance of being admitted, *not* the academic interest you genuinely want to study after you get in. I wish admissions worked in a way where you got rewarded for a sincere proclamation of your love for economics. As someone who loves economics, I really do. Sadly, this is not how the system works.

This doesn't mean you should go and spend all your high school years on physics and then declare love for art history or psychology. Your optimization is as follows: you want to choose the most niche, unpopular major possible for a given university subject to it being credible that you are genuinely interested in studying it and are qualified from your existing activities to be studying it.

Although my memory is getting a little foggy, I believe I applied for English to Yale, government at Harvard, financial engineering at Columbia and Princeton, English at Stanford and the Huntsman Program (a business degree and an international studies degree combined) for the University of Pennsylvania. All of these majors were reasonable given my high school achievements and activities. At the time I applied, I was relatively sure I was going to study economics and try and break into Wall Street, but I reasoned that I should really not just go and tick economics everywhere. The strategy proved to be successful and, thousands of admitted students later, it is an empirical reality that major selection is critically important.

I don't particularly like the US system and the gymnastics it requires. When it comes to UK universities, you apply to the university *and* the course. So given I wanted to study economics at Cambridge, I applied for economics. Candidates have to declare what degree they want to study (or *read* as it is called at Oxbridge) from the outset, and if they apply for it, they have to study it. This takes the gaming out of major selection and lets candidates focus on showcasing what they actually want to study.

You, however, need to be a champion of the convoluted system, not another victim, so here are some clear steps you need to take.

First, research what majors a school has a core competency in that may not necessarily be well known by prospective applicants. For example, Harvard has a folklore and mythology major).[3] Hardly any universities offer an undergraduate major in this area. If you have some vague interest in this field, you could build a very compelling application for Harvard by developing a set of persuasive extracurriculars and academic pursuits based on this theme. Harvard knows it has a brilliant department in this area, so is likely to be excited to find prospective applicants who have done their research, want to study this area, and submit it in their application. This is great if it could relate to you. It is super niche, but it is a compelling way to distinguish yourself from the tsunami of economics applicants.

Second, take your academic interests one level deeper. I meet many students who like economics or computer science. If you like economics, explore one of the subfields— game theory, behavioral economics, development economics. If you genuinely explore economics, you will quickly find out there are many niches you could devote your entire career to if you wanted to. A small amount of focused online coursework, summer research, independent studies, or clubs focused on these subfields helps to build your credibility as someone who knows what they are talking about in a given discipline.

Rather than declaring your love for computer science, why not artificial intelligence? Artificial intelligence uses computer science and statistics and focuses on adaptive algorithms to make decisions that generally get better over time. Even better, what about artificial intelligence (AI) ethics? What happens when millions of people lose their manual jobs because AI algorithms can do them better than they can and it creates substantial inequality?

If you built a candidacy on the niche of AI ethics and took coursework such as AP Computer Science, online coursework such as Justice by Michael Sandel and Andrew Ng's famous machine learning class on Coursera, attended a futurist conference that addressed issues like singularity, and took a Yale Young Global Scholars class in literature, philosophy, and culture, you would be substantially more interesting than a student with a generic interest in computer science.

Rather than loving biology (as a wave of pre-medicine applicants do), how about marine biology? As I write this, I spoke to a boy in Shanghai today who is doing some exciting activities from Blackfish Public Screenings to joining PETA to online coursework in marine biology to AP Biology to advanced diving certificates to establish his interest in marine biology. Advancing from a generic biology interest to marine biology puts you in a much less competitive crowd because you can now articulate to an admissions officer a much more interesting and differentiated academic plan.

Third, never declare yourself "undeclared." Imagine if you wanted to raise money for your company from amazing investors. You turn up for the big meeting. They stare at you in anticipation and tell you to begin your pitch. You stand up in your fancy suit.

"I don't know what company I want to build yet, but I am awesome, so back me and I will figure it out."

Ninety-nine percent of the time this pitch gives you zero chance.

Unless you've already built a billion-dollar company and your approach is backed up by the fact that you've made so much money that any investor would feel like they just can't go wrong, pitching somebody no direction, no clear vision, no plan is utterly uninspiring.

Applying to a US university and saying you are undecided is just as uninspiring. Admissions officers get up every day to try and predict who will go on to accomplish incredible things and who won't. They want to bet on vision, purpose, direction, execution ability, and your track record. If, after 14 years of schooling, you don't have enough thirst for a single discipline to declare an academic interest, something is probably wrong.

In reality, many applicants, myself included, are not sure what they want to do when they get into university. The beauty of the US liberal arts system is that you can switch your major, try some different fields, and find your academic trajectory once you get in. Although this is true and the word *undeclared* might align with this way of thinking, it is a very bad strategy for the admissions process.

Find a pathway that you are relatively interested in, that is credible and ties back to your activities and proven academic interests (and avoid the common majors), and make this the focus of your application. Declare a strategy, show the admissions officer you have some vision and clear interests, and go for it.

Declaring undecided doesn't make you seem trendy or philosophical. Most curious academic students have too many potential majors, so they aren't sure what they should focus on. In that case, you can list many different academic interests and elaborate more in your additional information section. But don't, whatever you do, declare undecided.

Some students do get in declaring undecided but they face an uphill battle compared to those students who articulate a clear academic plan and pitch that in their application process. It is okay if your hypothesis of your college career is not fully formed, but you need to have a well-researched hypothesis that you can articulate easily and persuasively.

I see thousands of the world's most talented students every year and generally the smartest, most academically qualified high school students often have very advanced views of what they want to do in university and in their careers. A clear vision of the future is generally highly correlated with strong success. It is hard for most people to find burning motivation to push through grueling academics and an array of extracurriculars with absolutely no vision for what the future holds beyond getting into a university. It is okay to have too many interests (however, for your application, we want to tone that down and articulate only a central one or two), but having no interests at all is a bad strategy.

Your application needs to tie one or two central themes and you need to articulate a clear academic game plan for college (while once again avoiding the common majors) so that an admissions officer can extrapolate and imagine what amazing things you can go on to accomplish in the future (and they can willingly and proudly claim you as an alum). Give your admissions officer a crystal ball and tell them what you want them to see in it.

Chapter 5

The Extracurricular Results/Effort Ratio

What It Is, How It Works, and Why It Matters

Ultimately, your career is a game of time optimization. What is the best you can do given the time you have?

High school is exactly the same. Most high schoolers have fairly comparable available hours. There are obvious exceptions. Students from disadvantaged backgrounds may have to work to support their family, care for their siblings, and engage in other activities that limit their available hours. (These obligations are incredibly important and a very noble use of a young person's time. They say a lot about the character of the student themselves, which is, and should be, an important part of an admissions officer's assessment of that student.) But here, in this chapter, we will make the admittedly flawed assumption that every high schooler has roughly the same amount of hours on the clock.

Next, we assume that the world has enough ambitious high school students who are willing to do practically anything to land a spot at a treasured, globally prestigious university. These students are generally willing to put in almost all available hours (and I say "almost" because every young person needs to factor in some downtime), beyond sleeping and eating to pursuits necessary to get into their dream colleges.

Once you are competing at this level you encounter the core strategic dilemma. How do you best use your time?

Many students have comparable levels of ambition, hustle, and work ethic, yet some get in and some fail. One of the primary reasons for this is time allocation. Every academic pursuit, every extracurricular activity, almost everything you do in high school can take vastly differing amounts of time and result in vastly different outcomes. Some students get sucked into time traps that burn a lot of their useful hours on activities that have no tangible impact on their college application. Others effectively navigate the time traps and plow their time into productive activities that admissions officers highly respect and value, and in doing so, get ahead of the competition and get accepted.

A quick story to make the point. In high school, one of my fierce competitors was pursuing an ATCL Diploma in Violin. This is a diploma offered by the prestigious Trinity College London.[1] This diploma required him to pursue a string of violin grades (Grade 1 to Grade 8) and because much of the knowledge required to be accomplished in the violin accumulates over time, it required a strong foundation. Over the course of about seven years, getting the diploma took approximately 300 hours. This is probably conservative if you factor in travel time to lessons, recitals, practice hours, lessons, and other associated commitments. I didn't really have much talent for music. Playing the violin looked confusing to say the least, and I hadn't had much success with guitar, so frankly it seemed like it would be a disaster. I looked around and saw legions of students who had begun the violin at young ages. This was not a competition I was going to win.

I decided to pursue an ATCL Diploma in Communications.[2] This is a diploma also offered by Trinity College London. It tests your ability to deliver professional speeches in various settings and is designed to make you a more effective communicator. I loved debating and thought this sounded genuinely useful. Communication skills, unlike violin, do not have the same kind of prerequisites. I practiced speaking every day and competitive debating helped hone my ability to give speeches under high pressure environments. As a result, I was able to skip virtually all the grades and jump into Grade 6 and then Grade 8 and then pursue the ATCL Diploma. All up, I spent about 30 hours getting my ATCL Diploma (including about 15 1:1 lessons with my instructor Jacqui). I passed the diploma with strong grades.

I spent 30 hours getting an ATCL Diploma in Communications. My competitor spent ~300 hours getting his diploma in violin. Ironically, my diploma is rarer than the violin diploma because so many students study violin, so potentially not only was my diploma much less time consuming but it was also more interesting to admissions officers.

Further, my competitor didn't even enjoy the violin very much but had been pushed into it at an early age by his parents. I had completed a comparable qualification in 10% of the time—and I enjoyed doing it! Fast-forward to today and the fellow dropped the violin many years ago. I continue to communicate in high-stakes environments on a weekly basis.

In this case, I chose an activity that enabled me to get a highly regarded qualification, recognized by admissions officers, that synced to my future needs, was genuinely interesting, and was highly efficient in terms of hours required. This is an example of a slam dunk extracurricular pursuit.

In the 270 odd extra hours I had up my sleeve from not running the violin gauntlet, I was able to take many additional A-Level subjects, boosting my academic candidacy and probably spent a little bit more time with my wonderful high school girlfriend. The violin (and the piano) are classic examples of a time trap. Although very few students succeed with these highly time-intensive instruments, in general, it is a pitfall of pain, misery, arguments at home, and unhelpful in terms of your college applications.

With each activity, you need to calculate the results/ effort ratio. I define results as the tangible outcomes that an admissions officer would care about. By all means, not everything during high school needs to matter for college, but most students are thinking strategically about all their activities. If you are doing the activity partially because it will help you when you submit your university applications, make sure you are clear on what results you are going to get. Results need to be specific: leadership roles, ranked awards that mean something, placings in regional or national teams, the number of people you have affected, the amount of money you raised, a grade or a certificate. You can't just tip time into an activity and get no results because it is ultimately the result that college admissions officers care about and evaluate.

Now going back to our friends at the admissions office. They may tell you to do what you like, but Harvard gave me no credit for my hundreds of hours spent playing Call of Duty or Yu-Gi-Oh or binge-watching action and horror movies. Harvard didn't give me credit for assembling

Warhammer armies or hanging out with my friends. By all means, do the fun things as well, but when you are on the college admissions candidacy grind, you need to know what results you are getting from the time you are investing. Later in life you need to worry about the return on money you invest, but in high school (when you have no money to invest!), your most precious resource is your time. So get those returns!

I define effort as the time invested as well as the emotional pain and anguish (or the potential joy) of an activity. I used to hate my guitar lessons—and I mean passionately *hate* them. In fact, I hated them so much I just stopped turning up to my music lessons in Year 6. This happened so many times that my guitar teacher would come hunting for me at morning tea or lunch time when I was supposed to be seeing him, and I would hide like a chicken embarrassed he would find me and haul me into that mind-numbingly boring practice room.

For me, guitar wasn't just an activity that took time but I really, really disliked it. The effort was not just the hours involved for lessons and practice (not that I ever practiced as I hated it so much), but the psychological pain associated with the activity. When I knew I had to attend a guitar-related activity, I would dread it all day and count the hours until I had to do it. These types of pain-inducing activities you genuinely don't enjoy create friction in your life beyond just the hours involved. They make you more tired, unmotivated, and unhappy. As a result, even if you are being pragmatic and trying to fully optimize for college admissions, you really shouldn't do activities that you genuinely don't enjoy.

Combining results and effort, you get a really effective results/effort ratio. Obviously, this can't be calculated precisely, but it gives you a prioritization framework you can use to evaluate whether an activity is a good one to pursue or not.

One time in high school I signed up to be in the Glee Club. I was cast in a minor role (imagine a guard but it could have been a tree it was so trivial). I had to attend about five full Sunday mandatory rehearsals, burning my precious weekends, removing me from fun activities and academics. After endless rehearsals, getting yelled at (at least once) for being late, spending eight minutes of an entire Sunday saying my meaningless few lines, and otherwise waiting around for hours watching the much more talented leads do their key scenes again and again and again, it dawned on me. This is a total time waster.

Never again did I participate in theatre or school productions.

My time in Glee Club wasn't like the fun TV show. For me at least it was dull, uninteresting, and a real waste of time for someone cast in a vague support role. The results/effort ratio was terrible. This was no ATCL Diploma in Communications.

Many students make the mistake of trying to compete in the most competitive extracurricular activities. I've trained students through Crimson to be VEX World Robotics champions, Gold Medalists in the various Math, Chemistry, Physics, Informatics, Economics Olympiads, win the biggest awards at ISEF, get into MIT RSI,[3] intern for the United Nations, conquer global competitions, and all kinds of other epic achievements. Students look at these and think that the results side of the equation will be amazing if they get in, but the problem is the last part if they get in.

A very, very small share of students can tackle the most competitive competitions of all and reign supreme. I got into virtually all the best universities in high school and I had no Mathematics Olympiad medals. When I initially tried the Mathematics Olympiad, I realized that frankly I could not compete with these students. The kids that go on to win the golds in the Mathematics Olympiads are like the Navy Seals of high school academics. These kids are like the Rock of action stars. If they were extreme sportspeople, they would be the ones squirrel suit diving off major office buildings and avoiding what seems to be certain death.

Mathematics Olympiad, for basically everyone reading this, is a time trap. The time required to actually do well is incredibly high. Many of the best students are accelerating in mathematics from a very young age. The chance you can actually win is very low. If you are reading this and you are 10, I feel a bit better about supporting you in giving this a crack. But in most cases, do not try. It is a total time drain. The results part of the equation is not going to look good because you won't win a medal. The time part of the equation is going to be painful as you pour hours into abstract geometry problems.

You need to be willing to swallow your ego and ditch time traps and plow your time into areas you can effectively compete in. In high school, I was one of the best debaters within my city and in my last year of high school, I won three of the major tournaments with my two debate partners. Heading into Harvard, I figured I was a pretty good debater. I joined the Harvard debate team and began immediately hearing about two people. One fellow freshman, Bo, was the highest ranked debater in the world in high school. Another freshman, Fanele, was the second highest ranked debater in the world in high school. Unsurprisingly, these two partnered up to form a team. I went along to a Boston University debate tournament in the first weekend and my debate partner, Dhruva, and I ended up winning third in the tournament. The winners were Bo and Fanele. I thought about this and quickly realized, no matter how much I pour in, these two have already clocked more hours of debating practice in high school than I could realistically catch up on and they are only going to get better. They've partnered with each other.

Extrapolating, I realized that I could commit my precious Harvard weekends to debating and be beaten again and again by Bo and Fanele, or I could find my own race to run. I never debated again since that Boston tournament, switched to finance, and became one of the best finance students at Harvard. I went on to land an exclusive internship at Tiger, one of the world's best hedge funds, as a college student, which was unheard of. This was all because frankly, I wasn't good enough to win at debating and had to find my own race to run. Fortunately, the race I chose paid slightly better.

At Crimson, one of our values is "student outcome obsessed." I launched Crimson so that I could be a major driver in student opportunity. I had, and still have, a constant burning passion to want to help talented and hardworking students reach their ultimate college admissions goals. You need that same type of focus in high school—but for you this means lifting yourself above those around you. Only one kid from your school is generally getting into Harvard (unless you attend Phillips Exeter Academy or some of the other leading schools). The world's best universities can sit back dispassionately and wait for everyone to compete in high school and pick out the kids who come out on top.

Fortunately, you are going to choose the right race to run. Avoid Mathematics Olympiad. Avoid violin and piano. Focus on niche activities that you can totally dominate within your high school, region, city, or country. I'd rather you are the world curling champion than being in your high school's second-best US football team. I'd prefer you are the national Latin champion than a mediocre French speaker.

As an entrepreneur, the market rewards people who build dominant, niche-conquering businesses. People are happy to back people who are demonstrated winners in a game, even if it is initially a small game. As a high school student, universities reward individuals who can prove they can win or thrive at a given domain of expertise. They figure that if you can compete and shine against fellow high schoolers in a certain activity, you probably have the determination it requires to sustain excellence in their college. This assumption is generally correct.

Apply the results/effort ratio; choose the niche races, activities, and academic pursuits where possible; and compete where you can play to win, not participate. Apply this rule religiously and you'll end up after four years of high school well ahead of your peers who aren't strategically time optimizing.

Chapter 6

Not A School Leader?
Go Build Your
Own Empire

The best universities place a big premium on leadership. Of the 70+ students I've sent to Harvard and Stanford, a reasonable chunk were head of their student government. Being elected head boy, head girl, school captain, or the equivalent role is an immediate signal to the university that you have strong support from teachers, the headmaster, your peers, and likely have strong communication skills, time management skills, and an ability to relate to a wide variety of stakeholders.

These are powerful characteristics. This is not silly. I've hired many staff members at Crimson who were formerly student leaders and, in general, the leadership traits demonstrated in high school often have some predictability of future success, at least to some extent.

In high school, I had two clear goals for my last year. I wanted to be Dux (Valedictorian) or the highest ranked academic student. I also aspired to be a head student. I was successful in the first category but missed out on the second. This was a bit of a blow to my college admissions game plan, but I had anticipated that I only had a small shot at landing the leadership role I aspired for. As a result, I had begun to create my own leadership roles.

There are broadly two types of leadership roles we discuss at Crimson. The first are institutional leadership roles: head of the student government, captain of a sports team, board trustee. These are the kinds of positions that you are voted or elected into and already exist as part of some organizational infrastructure. These roles generally have clear responsibilities and multiple people vying for them.

The second type of leadership role is the entrepreneurial leadership role. This is when a student creates their own club or initiative. In launching their own initiative, they are by default the founder or the captain or the club president. At high school, I launched a number of initiatives, from my student newspaper (*The King's Echo*), to a youth-for-youth safe drinking campaign called Don't Stand By, Stand Up. I created a Model United Nations club as well as a student company called Number 8 Technologies, which provided iPad stands for cars (when the iPad first came out!), so parents could use maps while driving.

One of the defining characteristics of Crimson's admitted students to Ivy League schools and other great institutions is the broad array of entrepreneurial leadership roles they create. These roles are brilliant in general because they don't rely on someone electing you to the position. You can create your own initiative in white space and design the club you want to lead.

Most high schools are somewhat friendly to the creation of new clubs, as long as you don't cause too much trouble for school administrators and have a reasonable reputation within the school. At our online high school, Crimson Global Academy, we actively encourage students to launch their own clubs and initiatives. It is a brilliant way to get your first taste of leadership, organization, and what it takes to drive a group of people behind a common goal.

A strong aspiring applicant to the world's best universities needs to construct an array of activities with a diversified portfolio of options. If you stake your university candidacy on being voted head student and you fail, you're in a bit of a perilous situation. Instead, take your core interests or themes you are building your university candidacy on and start creating initiatives related to this focus point early (from as early as Grade 9 onwards).

At Crimson, we have refined the process of supporting young students to ideate these initiatives, develop what an initial starting point could look like, and launch them (each of our students has a team member dedicated solely to extracurriculars). Many students will fail to think of an idea by themselves, and others will fail to have the courage and conviction to go ahead and actually develop it. With strong support and a clear, achievable vision they can push from milestone to milestone and develop initiatives that have genuine impact.

Let me give you some concrete examples of what some of our previous students have done so you can see what this looks like in practice.

One of my students who attended Caltech and now works at Goldman Sachs launched a charity initiative focused on raising awareness for cerebral palsy. She arranged an in-person event that was well attended with strong speakers who could help the audience understand what life was like with this condition while also raising revenue through donations and ticket sales.

Another of my students, who went to the University of Pennsylvania and studied digital, media, and design, designed a water-filtration system. He used computer-aided design to develop a prototype and then worked with a local professor to turn the visuals into something deployable.

I also worked with a student who got into New York University's Stern School of Business and then went into investment banking. She arranged an event called Unite for UNICEF. At the event, food was prepared for less than $US1.50/day, which is the international poverty line. Tickets were sold for $US20+ and the audience was wowed by the creativity of the simple food developed by a local chef. Local politicians and speakers from UNICEF came along to articulate the importance of various child poverty initiatives locally and in developing countries. The event raised several thousand dollars and received prominent media coverage within the Chinese community. The student then went on to launch a network of UNICEF clubs across schools in her country scaling her impact and passion for the charity significantly.

One of my students who got into Stanford and is now working at Silver Lake (the billion-dollar global technology investment firm), created a gender equality club focused on raising awareness for the lack of representation of female politicians in some areas of the US government. She achieved significant membership within her school community and attended a number of prominent marches.

Another of my students who went to Harvard and is now an investment banker arranged a significant fundraiser for Indigenous Australian students to receive support to attend a national choral program to support their passion for arts. The event raised several thousand, featured local politicians and nonprofit leaders, and involved some awe-inspiring performances of young magicians.

There was also the student who went to Stanford and worked at McKinsey. He organized a start-up pitch competition in which teams of students could pitch a business idea to a panel of judges from a local business incubator and a network of angel investors. This competition raised awareness for entrepreneurship as a career path for young high schoolers and helped them to develop business strategy ideas.

One of my students who got into Stanford and studied computer science launched a multiple-choice quiz mobile application to help his fellow students practice for their high school exams.

My students have launched mobile applications, viral petitions, social media campaigns, school clubs, impactful charities, online newspapers, YouTube channels, podcasts, and all sorts of other initiatives. These initiatives have significant value in the eyes of the admissions office because they show that the student has an ability to act, make things happen, articulate a vision, and has entrepreneurial acumen.

Critics point to funny examples of students building Habitat for Humanity houses in far-flung parts of Africa and other extreme projects. Virtually all of the students I've seen admitted to the world's most prestigious universities in recent years have completed projects built on core interests they have, within their local community, that cost nothing to create or develop.

A strong applicant will generally have about three to five entrepreneurial leadership roles in their profile. These roles by themselves do not have significant value. Starting a club and doing nothing with it isn't going to fool anybody. If anything, superficial activities can be detrimental to an otherwise strong profile because admissions officers can usually tell if you are stretching to find something of value to share with them in your application journey.

By contrast, you want to be meticulous and ask yourself about what you can actually achieve that will make a clear, tangible impact on the lives of your school, students, or community. How big is your group? How active are the members? Have you built a serious website to attract new members? Do you meet regularly and achieve sufficient recognition in your school community that your peers would respect what you have built? Are your members learning something of value from the meetings? Have you been able to recruit a group of advisors, speakers, or mentors to support the initiative and bridge knowledge gaps you may have? Have you established a formal leadership structure so the organization will keep developing when you have left your high school? Have you been able to raise funding or sponsorship to support your case? These are just some of the questions you need to ask to make sure what you are building is of real entrepreneurial value.

When you create your entrepreneurial leadership roles, you generally want to avoid areas that are well-trodden. Creating another Model United Nations club or a debate club if your school already has one isn't really helping anyone. One of my students launched the first artificial intelligence club in his city at his respected local school. He was able to organize various industry participants to speak to his members so they could build a genuine understanding of the key challenges in the field of AI. He convinced school stakeholders to get behind the club and share it with more students than he could recruit. He took online courses such as Harvard's CS50[1] and Andrew Ng's machine learning course[2] and read books such as *AI Superpowers*[3] (my favorite book) to make sure he had a working knowledge of the field so that he could be a useful resource to his more elementary peers who were just getting started.

I really liked this initiative because it related to a core aspect of his candidacy, was of genuine interest to him, had never been done before, was highly topical, and could meaningfully change the career interests of his peers. It was in a topic area that wasn't well understood by a traditional high school that may at best offer some computer science classes. When the student graduates, he will have left behind a sustainable leadership structure so the club should endure beyond his time. These are all the hallmarks of a powerful leadership project.

Entrepreneurial projects are fantastic because you don't need to be the stereotypical leader to be able to do them. I wasn't the most confident speaker in high school and I didn't have a natural instinct for leadership in which I could rally a room. Focusing on some niche activities I cared about, such as creating a safer environment for my peers, launching a newspaper that used my writing skills and gave my peers something interesting to read in the mornings, and creating a business, enabled me to start to develop some leadership chops and get the ball rolling.

I firmly believe that leadership can be trained and developed. Some people may naturally be more inclined toward leadership than others, but time and time again I've witnessed students who are 12 or 13 and struggle to make eye contact. At that point they are painfully shy but they develop incredibly by the end of high school.

I remember vividly one of my early students who joined us when she was about 14 years old. She was incredibly ambitious but shy and averted her eyes when I made eye contact with her. She was jittery but clearly talented. She started small, participating in some local Model United Nations clubs before launching her own UNICEF club. She represented her country on an international Model United Nations delegation and went on to be the head of the student government by the end of high school. Today, she has almost finished her Stanford degree. Lots of people told me in high school that I didn't seem like a very natural leader (and I would have agreed with them), but today I have the privilege of managing more than 400 employees who rely on my strategy and vision every day. Leadership can be trained and developed.

US universities put significant weight on leadership because they are trying to pick winners. They want to admit students who will go on to create unicorn companies or run for political office or play a significant role in their local communities. Show them you have the potential to develop an idea, scale it, and rally your community behind it.

Create your own future and focus on entrepreneurial leadership initiatives at the beginning. If you begin in the early waves of intermediate or high school, you can even build a brand as a student leader within your school early, which will help you lock down institutional leadership roles later as my initially shy Stanford admit did.

Chapter 7

Don't Be Fooled

Recommendation Letters Are Audit Trails

One of the crazy things about applying to a US university for your undergraduate degree is that almost nothing about your extracurriculars on the application is actually audited.

When I applied and was accepted to Stanford Business School for my master's in business administration, a verification service called a bunch of my former employers to check I had worked where I said I had worked and earned what I said I had earned. They also requested verified copies of my undergraduate transcripts. This is a brilliant system because they let applicants apply for business school and then decide if they want to admit them based on what they have written on their application. After deciding that an applicant looks promising, and offering them a place in their program, they then pay a verification service to verify their candidacy. This means they aren't forcing every single applicant to pay for the often expensive verification services, but are confident that when people turn up for class in the fall, they actually did what they said they did.

For undergraduate applications, this is not the case. You will submit various academic grades that are generally verified by your high school, but unfortunately, none of your high school extracurricular activities are actually verified in any way. This means that a student could theoretically go and claim they have done anything (like launch a start-up and raise $US1 million from undisclosed investors), and potentially convince an admissions officer to admit them based on something that isn't real. This is obviously highly unethical and it disadvantages honest applicants who just share their authentic activities with precise language.

The good thing is that most admissions officers have various ways to sniff out the truth. First, students up until recently had to submit SAT or ACT scores. These scores are generally, with only a few exceptions (as Rick Singer showed us), reliable indicators of a student's ability. They assess mathematics and English and ultimately provide colleges a powerful guide as to your potential for academic success.

You may have fantastical extracurriculars (that could be real or not), but if you didn't have a credible standardized test score (usually 34+ for the ACT or 1500+ for the SAT), you would be hard-pressed to gain admission to a highly competitive US university. Generally the students with the highest test scores often have the strong extracurriculars as well, because they have a strong incentive to perform well across the board to become competitive for the best universities.

Additionally, admissions officers develop strong intuition for what is credible. Does the applicant describe some actual events that took place (one of my students did three Sunday beach cleanups with her sustainability group), or just vaguely refer to a sustainability club? Does the applicant refer to other members in the group and the size of the organization? Does the applicant have a website they can refer to so an admissions officer can dive a bit deeper if they want to and learn about the organization?

One of the most powerful ways, however, to verify the veracity of extracurriculars are the reference letters. These are the informal audit trails of the US undergraduate application process. When I was applying to universities, I had poured so much time into my extracurriculars that I was hell-bent on making sure I received strong credit for this work. As a result, I approached my referees Mr. Sapsworth, my advanced physics teacher, and Mr. Bean, my French teacher, and carved out all my activities into two categories (STEM and humanities broadly), giving both teachers a summary sheet of what I hoped they could reference.

Mr. Sapsworth was able to touch on my work in the International Young Physicist's Tournament, my role in New Zealand's Next Top Engineering Scientist, as well as various math competitions I was involved in. He did this on top of commenting on my academic success in physics, mathematics, and other STEM subjects. Mr. Bean was able to touch on my Duke of Edinburgh Gold Award,[1] my ATCL Diploma in Communications, my various tournament wins in debating, and strong academic performance in French and English. He was also a former teacher at Eton (one of the UK's most prestigious high schools with a top reputation for academics[2]), so was able to give context on my 10 A Levels and how that compared to the normal three to four.

My headmaster wrote my final reference and touched on the strong impact in our school community of my Don't Stand By, Stand Up safe drinking initiative in the wake of some tragedies in our school. He was also able to touch on the impact of a number of the clubs I had launched or led and role as a school leader.

The key lesson here is simple. Your reference letters for the best US universities should not only comment on your academic success. Obviously, you want to choose teachers who taught you in classes you did well in (scoring an A or equivalent in your curriculum), who can speak to your character, your impact on the classroom, and your peers. But you also want them to share, in significant detail, your extracurriculars and the impact they've had on the school community and beyond.

Harvard knows what the Mathematics Olympiad is, but Harvard can't know about the tangible impact of all your entrepreneurial leadership roles unless your teacher describes them. Harvard doesn't know what you actually did with the leadership roles you were given by your school— but they will if they are detailed with passion in that all-important letter of recommendation.

In other words, your references are your audit trail, and the fact that they can be long—600 words or more— provides your referees with a lot of space and time to pontificate on who you are and what you've actually done. The admissions officer should then be able to tell, across your own description of your activities on the Common Application (or the equivalent University of California or MIT processes), and your teacher references, precisely what you added to your school community and in turn what you'll contribute to their campus.

But remember, the references don't just help you. They can hurt you as well. If you claim you've launched a bunch of highly impactful clubs but your references don't reference them, it may raise concerns. If your student newspaper was actually so big, why doesn't your English teacher care enough to write about it? If you were a senior school leader and your counselor can't point to any initiatives that occurred during your tenure, were you actually doing anything of great significance?

Silence speaks volumes in college admissions.

In order to proactively build your reference trail, I recommend inviting a teacher to get involved in each of the school initiatives you launch. This means they are there from inception and witness your struggles launching the club or program and how it develops. They are emotionally committed to you as they see you invest time and energy into the growth of your organization.

If you choose carefully, you may find a teacher who really is passionate about what you are trying to create and can help you scale it faster. This teacher then becomes a natural candidate for a reference down the line when it is application time. It is worth noting that you can generally only submit three references to most universities, so ideally the teacher you ask to get involved is someone you already know, because if you're excelling in their class they can effectively cover both bases.

The other way to build your own audit trail for your entrepreneurial leadership roles is through the well-hidden "Additional Information" section.

Most applicants apply to US colleges through the Common Application platform. Other groups such as the Coalition Application have tried to offer alternatives in recent years, but the Common App platform is defiant and it doesn't seem like it is going to be dislodged anytime soon.

If you are applying to college through the Common Application system, you will find yourself typing in your 10 activities into the "Activities" section, and if you've been working hard in high school, you'll find yourself starved for words. You really don't have much space to articulate your activities (a measly 150 characters per activity!). You've poured so much time into these projects and you have only a feeble two sentences to articulate your work!

Not to worry. There is a section called "Additional Information" that many students miss but you won't. This enables you to use up to 650 additional words to add context to anything you like.

This is your gold mine.

For each of your entrepreneurial projects, you can articulate the impact you had in more precise detail. I also advise you to make sure you have a website for each of your projects. These websites (which can be created on WIX.com or other such platforms) should articulate the mission of your club, your members, what projects you have worked on, and have a contact form so that new members could potentially join. You may want to include photos of the events you have run and other related initiatives. The websites can then be linked in your additional information section so a curious admissions officer can dig a little deeper if need be and see what you have built in all its glory.

This section is also useful to list any other activities or achievements you have that you couldn't fit in the main body of the application. I recommend being as thorough as possible. If you blindly rank 100 applicants based on the length of their "Additional Information Section," generally the strongest applicants have the most thorough descriptions. Applicants who are struggling to fill their activity list may miss this section entirely or fill it with nothing of consequence. You, however, should aspire to be the student who is running out of words on even the "Additional Information Section"! This is the position most of our ambitious Crimson students find themselves in, and this is usually the sign of a job well done on the extracurricular front.

There are other ways to build external validation into your application. This is essential especially if you are from a school or country that universities are not so familiar with. If you attend an elite institution like Philips Andover, the guidance counsellor often has the power to literally call up the Harvard admissions office and recommend which students they think are a strong fit. Because the high school is so well known and was founded in 1778,[3] Harvard has had a long time to understand the nuances of the school and what the various achievements of the students are likely to mean.

But most high schools are not like this. For most of the world's high schools, getting a child into Harvard is a rare once in a decade occurrence. This means that generally your high school will not be well understood by most admissions officers.

Taking A Levels or Advanced Placement (AP) qualifications gives you well-understood certificates that showcase your academic competency. Taking formal extracurriculars, such as VEX Robotics and other courses, which have a longstanding track record, is also a good idea. Getting media coverage behind your initiatives helps. The media do their own (light) fact-checking process before they generally cover you. This means that when a local publication does a piece on your youth project or your new mobile app, it provides a signal to the university that what you are doing is likely to have substance.

I also recommend videos when possible. If you arrange a big fundraising event with notable local speakers, you as the master of ceremonies, a range of performances in an exciting venue, film it! Although most admissions officers may not want to watch a one-hour long video when they have thousands of applications to deal with, they will watch it if they are on the fence about you because seeing you in action may be enough to swing them to your side. Don't feel the need to use super professional video people. That's expensive and unnecessary. Do what you can to capture the moment, potentially borrowing some equipment from your school. Take the video and compress it so it is easy to render, host it on Google Drive or another platform, and attach the link in the additional information section.

Apply the audit trail framework wherever you can to add extra credibility to your application. Anything that isn't well understood or doesn't seem credible will be discounted and diminished. If you play music or create art to any reasonable standard, submit a portfolio that showcases your work. This can be developed over many years gradually and incrementally and gives the admissions office another lens through which they can understand you.

My clarinet skills were enough to get me into my high school's concert band, but were definitely not strong enough for a solo performance. I gave up on art when I was eight when a student in my art class laughed at my work and told me it was terrible. As much as it hurt at the time, there was a candidness to his words, and I abandoned that path early. I hope you have more musical or artistic skills than I do (which would not be hard!). If you do, add them to the application, bolster your audit trail, and let the admissions officers see it!

A final reflection for you on references and audit trails . . .

Many students ask teachers for recommendation letters and just hope for the best. Don't do this. No matter how close your teacher is to you and how much they like you, they don't have an encyclopedic memory of what you've done. They are busy, and although squeezing out your reference letter will be important to them, they will probably have to hash it out quickly in between classes and marking papers. Although they mean well, you don't want their lack of time to diminish your admissions odds, so make the reference letter process super easy for them by giving them a clear fact sheet.

This sheet should summarize all your key academic achievements you think are relevant for them to know as well as all the extracurriculars you want them to reference. Ultimately, they can write whatever they like, but if you give them a fact sheet, you give them easy access to the detail you want them to reference. It makes their life easier for them and gives you a stronger application.

Chapter 8

The Kingmakers
Here's How the Best of the Best Defeat the Rest of the Best of the Best

Although you can build your own entrepreneurial leadership roles, participate in your own niche extracurriculars, and find swim lanes you can dominate, it goes without saying that there is a small group of kingmaker activities.

If you do well in them, admission is almost guaranteed at a wide range of universities—and for good reason. These are exceptionally difficult things to pull off. For most applicants, these are time traps, but for the small portion of you reading this who have the kind of formidable academic talent to make these awards achievable, keep reading.

First up, we have the Olympiads. There are a number of major global Olympiads. The International Mathematics Olympiad (IMO)[1] is arguably the most prestigious of the science Olympiads. The first IMO was held in Romania in 1959. It has been held consistently since then. Teams from more than 100 countries compete. In designing the competition, it was decided that competitors are not expected to know aspects of advanced mathematics and so calculus, for example, is not needed to solve most problems. Areas such as geometry, combinatorics, and number theory are commonly tested.

The selection process for the International Mathematics Olympiad is grueling. In New Zealand, for example, students have to compete in the September Problems. This involves submitting written answers to a range of challenging mathematics questions. From there, a small group of students are chosen for a selection camp. At this camp, the highest performing five students are then selected to represent New Zealand at the International Mathematics Olympiad.

Math is particularly brutal to compete in because it is one of the main areas of academic acceleration that many students focus on at a young age. I see many students who are accelerated three to four years ahead of their age when they are younger by their ambitious parents (with hopefully some love for the subject). This kind of acceleration is natural in mathematics because it is a core subject you take as soon as you begin school. It is much rarer to see young students from other science disciplines, such as biology and chemistry, beginning these fields prior to high school (although I am seeing it more and more).

The combination of the prevalence of accelerated mathematics opportunities and the handful of kids selected in the national Mathematics Olympiad team makes for an incredibly competitive extracurricular activity. The race, however, is not over. Getting to the national team is impressive but what really matters is winning medals.

National teams go on to an exotic global location each year and compete at the International Mathematics

Olympiad and are awarded different levels of medals: bronze, silver, or gold. My gold medal award–winning Crimson alumni like Seyoon, who was 17th in the world in the International Mathematics Olympiad, had to make performing in this competition a major, nearly all-consuming, academic goal for many years to achieve this kind of excellence. Seyoon by the way just graduated from Princeton winning the school's coveted George B. Covington math prize. He also recently interned at Citadel, a leading quantitative trading Wall Street investment firm.

Any admissions officer knows that a medalist from the Mathematics Olympiad is likely to be an incredible asset to their student community. MIT is notorious for relentlessly following the Olympiads to scout their potential admits. They place so much weight on the rigor of the tournament in filtering the best of the best, that they're confident that if they admit the upper tier of students who made it through this academic juggernaut, they'll have found the cream of the crop. To be honest, they are right. Almost every Olympiad student I've seen through Crimson has been exceptionally talented and a very worthwhile recipient of a spot at a competitive university.

The value of a medal in the Mathematics Olympiad doesn't stop at just getting into an elite university. Many of the most prestigious Wall Street firms who focus on high-frequency trading or quantitative trading (using algorithms to make trading decisions in the stock market) like Jane Street love to hire the students who have achieved success in these competitions. They generally find this kind of incredible academic firepower is a strong predictor of individuals who can seek out profits in the stock market with systematic algorithms and financial models. As an example, one of our alumni, who won a silver medal in the International Mathematics Olympiad, went to Harvard University and then worked at prestigious trading firm D. E. Shaw and now Jane Street.

Mathematics isn't the only Olympiad talented students can consider. Other notable Olympiads include the Biology Olympiad,[2] the Chemistry Olympiad,[3] and the International Young Physicist's Tournament.[4] Without fail, virtually all my Olympiad medalists over the last eight years have secured offers to top-10 US universities as well as Oxford and Cambridge. One of our alumni, Zhong, who scored a silver medal in the Biology Olympiad, won a full scholarship to Duke University and was admitted as an international student to the California Institute of Technology. He went on to land an internship at Waymo, Google's leading autonomous driving car unit. He scored a perfect 4.0 GPA at Caltech (very difficult!) and was admitted into MIT. He now works at Tesla. Elon Musk evidently has a good eye for young talent.

Another incredible program is the MIT Research Science Institute.[5] This highly selective program, supported by the legendary Massachusetts Institute of Technology, is a favorite for highly academic Crimson students. Each year, the program takes approximately 70 students. RSI alumni arguably have the most mind-blowing chart in the world of college admissions. From 1984 to 2019, a full 33% of their alumni have ended up at Harvard, 22% have ended up at MIT, Stanford claims 10%, Princeton claims another 5%, Yale follows suit with 5%, Caltech takes 3%, and Duke 2%.[6]

An 80% chance over 35 years of being admitted to Harvard, MIT, Stanford, Yale, Princeton, Caltech, or Duke is incredible. MIT RSI looks for students who have a track record of performing incredible research as a high school student. The program is entirely subsidized so all costs are covered for attendees. During the five-week program, students complete original scientific research under the guidance of fantastic professors and facilities they rarely can access at high school. It is a unique opportunity for a high schooler, but also an incredible signal to an admissions officer that you are one of the world's leading young scientists.

I haven't yet met an RSI alumni who didn't receive at least one Ivy League offer. We are delighted every time one of our Crimson students gets into a Research Science Institute because we know that beyond having an amazing summer, our student has just achieved their college admissions dreams as well.

A final program that makes my highlight reel is the ISEF Regeneron International Science and Engineering Fair.[7] Known for many years as the "Intel Science Fair" before the sponsor changed, this event has more than $US4 million in prize money available to cover tuition grants, sponsorships, and other prizes for the high schoolers who can reign supreme. If you have an incredible science fair project, this is the ultimate place to exhibit it.

It is worth noting that the significant majority of students we have sent to the Ivy League and other leading universities over the last eight years didn't have Olympiad medals, RSI placements, or Intel Science Fair awards. Harvard alone has to admit around 2,000 kids/year. There simply aren't enough medalists to go around.

As a result, rest assured you do not need to win these awards to have a chance at getting in. In fact, one of the most perilous and ill-advised strategies I have seen, which is particularly prevalent in China and Korea, is persevering with these competitions as the exclusive focus even when it is clear to a dispassionate observer that it isn't going to end well. Self-awareness is required in this process in order to allocate time efficiently.

I remember giving the New Zealand September problems for the Mathematics Olympiad a good crack when

I was about 14 and attending a couple of Mathematics Olympiad lunchtime sessions with my old math teacher, May Meng. It became clear to me pretty soon that this was not going to be my game. I abandoned ship early and switched to debate, where I found a niche I could thrive in. Harvard may have liked me slightly better if I did bring a Mathematics Olympiad medal along with some debate trophies, but it turned out okay in the end.

For most of you reading, avoid the time trap early, recognize if you cannot compete in these extracurriculars, and find your own domains to excel in. I've seen curling champions, e-sports professionals, a student who made hundreds of thousands by running Minecraft servers, a dentistry spelling bee champion, world Excel champions—the list goes on. Find your niche and dominate it. If Mathematics Olympiad is your niche, please call me and I'd like to be your first investor in your hedge fund. Otherwise, stay clear of the Olympiads like the plague.

Chapter 9

It's All Optional!

What the New "Test Optional" Universe Means to College Admissions

Now we've trekked through what you can and should add to your application, it may be time to discuss what you should but don't strictly have to include. I'm talking about the new test optional universe created, or at least given a good shove along by, COVID-19.

When I applied to Harvard, Yale, Princeton, Stanford, and a range of other universities, I was very focused on making sure I had strong standardized test scores. My high school had previously had limited success with US university admissions, so I wanted to make sure I had achieved well in some solid international benchmarks that were well understood.

I worked hard to get a high SAT score and also took six SAT Subject Tests. I wanted to showcase my academic skills across a wide range of subjects from Biology, Chemistry, and Physics to Mathematics 2, English Literature, and

French. The Subject Tests were out of 800 and took only an hour, but provided universities a clear standard of insight into my ability level across different fields.

During COVID-19, as test centers around the world were shut down again and again and students found it difficult to actually sit the standardized tests that for years played a critical role in admissions, universities had to make bold decisions. By the early deadline in November 2020, all the Ivy League universities had committed to go test optional. This meant that students didn't have to submit either an SAT or an ACT score if they didn't want to. Some students cheered. Many more were left bewildered and confused.

The call for the abolition of standardized tests has grown in recent years as clear empirical evidence has demonstrated that income and standardized test achievement were highly correlated. Critics argue that having standardized testing means that the admissions process skews toward higher income students. I don't necessarily have a strong view on this, but I do have strong views on what you need to do to get into college in the wake of this seismic shift.

First, optional means compulsory in the land of competitive college admissions. If you ever have the opportunity to write an optional essay, write it. If you ever have the opportunity to take an optional interview, take it. If you ever can submit an optional portfolio, do it.

Admissions officers have the challenging job of sorting through tens of thousands of applicants swiftly and therefore have to make quick filtering decisions. They inevitably need ways of sorting people. This is why the SAT and the ACT were so brilliant for many schools. If you were Harvard, you could cut a line through everyone with a 1440 or below and generally,[1] with limited regrets, have cut down a huge amount of your work. Universities could publish their historical SAT percentiles of achievement and candidates could self-filter and not bother applying to universities that were wildly out of reach.

For as long as these universities allow you to submit standardized tests, you should do your best to score highly in them and submit them. For years, I've heard the odd parent tell me their child doesn't "test well." Although I completely understand and feel for those with learning disabilities who sadly have to struggle in a test-centric world, the academic process—rightly or wrongly—is one that relies on exam after exam after exam. Admissions officers care a lot about your performance in academic assessments. It is possible to get into Harvard and other great institutions without submitting a standardized test, but you are fighting an uphill battle.

When a candidate applies to university, there are very few factors that are unquestionable facts. You may be the highest ranked student at your high school but in reality, how competitive is your high school? How does your school's curriculum actually compare to other peer institutions? What do all these extracurriculars actually mean?

The SAT and the ACT provide a single score that is standardized worldwide that enables an individual in Taiwan to be compared to one in Moscow to one in New Zealand to one in San Francisco.

The removal of the SAT and ACT is primarily designed to help low-income, disadvantaged students who may not be able to get adequate preparation to sit these tests. If you come from a high school that has a high proportion of people taking standardized tests, you really need to be taking the test unless your performance will be disastrous. To understand why, we can consult some basic game theory.

Imagine you are applying to Harvard and you have a perfect 1600 in the SAT (like our indigenous New Zealand student Sam Taylor who is actually now at Harvard).[2] Do you submit your score? Absolutely! You will move hell or highwater to submit that score. You are desperate to show the admissions officer that you are a standardized testing machine and nailed the test.

Now imagine you scored a 1550 in the SAT. Do you submit your score? This is above the average score of an accepted Harvard student. That sounds good. It is hard for anyone to criticize a 1550. This shows you are in the upper echelons of mathematics and English assessment. You submit it.

Next, imagine you scored a 1350 in the SAT. Do you submit your score to Harvard? 1350 is way below Harvard's average admitted score of 1520. No way! You want to hide that score and make sure Harvard never sees it.

What does this mean?

Game theoretically, any student who scores a 1520 or above is likely to submit their score to Harvard. It doesn't hurt them and probably helps them. However, if you don't submit your score, this means that you scored below 1520 in general. On average, using the conditional probability formula of Professor Blitzstein (my Harvard Stat 110 teacher), you have to ask what is the average score of the students who didn't want to submit their score to Harvard.

That score is probably in the 1300–1400 range. This means that if you go to a school in which most students actually apply to Harvard but you don't submit your score, they will assume your score is in the ~1350 range. That is going to lead to a decisive rejection (unless you have something extremely promising going for you like an Olympic medal in your back pocket).

Unfortunately, as long as the SAT and ACT are optional, you as a serious aspiring applicant need to study for it intensively, sit it, and submit your score (unless you are scoring 1350 or below).

This will not change even if only a small share of aspiring applicants to Harvard take it. It will only change if only a small share of actually admitted Harvard students take it. Until only ~15% or so of Harvard's admitted students are taking standardized tests and you have good reason to avoid them, you need to take them. If the SAT and ACT are literally removed from the admissions process, you can then avoid them entirely, but until then, game theory suggests you need to work hard and submit your SAT or ACT score.

Test optional admissions have created some interesting results. Applicant numbers have surged.

Previously, your SAT score might deter you from applying to your dream universities. Applicants are often overconfident and believe that their story may be unique enough to swing an admissions officer, even if their academic grades don't quite do them justice. With the removal of compulsory testing, there is nothing stopping a student from shipping an application to their dream universities.

Naturally, the most prestigious universities saw a big surge in the 2020/21 (first COVID-19 test-optional) admissions round. More than 57,000 students applied for the Harvard College's Class of 2025.[3] This was a 42% surge in applications compared to the class of 2024. Similar surges have been seen across the Ivy League and other major universities. The good news for you is many of these extra applicants aren't necessarily the strongest quality because many of them would have ordinarily self-selected out of applying. However, many of these extra applicants may indeed have something compelling about them. For every overzealous high schooler who wants to apply to every Ivy League school, there are students who are sadly dissuaded from applying outside of their state or to their reach schools by weak college counseling.

With the surge of applications, many of the admissions officers I have spoken to have also reported surges in fraud. I have discussed the need for an audit trail that helps an admissions officer verify the quality of your extracurriculars and school contributions. There has never been a greater need for this than now, as admissions officers find themselves spending significantly more time trying to figure out what all the opaque activities students are listing actually mean.

In a world where they don't have as much hard standardized testing data to go on, it is even more crucial that their assessment of an applicant's extracurriculars are robust. Given many students no longer have to report standardized tests that would have instantly eliminated them from the race, unethical, enterprising students are doctoring their extracurriculars in the hopes that their activities are not properly checked and taken at face value. Even the most well-resourced admissions offices are finding themselves stretched thin as they have to do more and more fact checking. Last year, Harvard and the rest of the Ivy League universities, who have arguably some of the most well-resourced admissions offices in the world, had to push back their admissions release dates by roughly a week in the wake of the surge in applications.[4]

Finally, with the removal of compulsory standardized testing (including the abolition of SAT Subject Tests, which were dropped by the College Board's testing schedule in 2021[5]), the need for other academic signals is growing.

As an applicant, you need to be taking more Advanced Placement assessments or more A Levels (the British equivalent). I am seeing my students taking more and more subjects in response to the void left behind by the original standardized testing focus. This isn't bad. Generally, a comprehensive high school curriculum like the A Levels is a more thorough learning experience than a generic mathematics and English aptitude test. The A Levels assess a student through long-form essays, short-form paragraph answers, as well as multiple-choice questions. The correlation between the best students and the best results tends to be higher the more varied the forms of assessment because it becomes harder to game these factors.

The famous Korean Hagwon, or "cram schools,"[6] that notoriously can occasionally produce 1550+ SAT scores out of students who can hardly speak English can no longer perform their black magic when the examination assessment gets more comprehensive.

Having studied the SAT for many years myself, I thought I was at the top of my game until I spent some time in Seoul. I met an SAT instructor who earned about $US500,000+/year running small-group instruction for ambitious local Korean students. He had studied the SAT English test structure so closely that he had established a withering array of tricks. If a question ended in a certain format, the answer is unlikely to be X, Y, or Z. If a question is testing this concept, the answer will usually start with A or B.

What appeared to be an English test had been decomposed into a web of structured rules that could be memorized and applied with impressive results. I personally like a system a lot better when the students scoring incredibly well in English assessments have to actually write comprehensive essays to showcase their aptitude!

The growth in demand for additional subjects has put significant pressure on high schools that often have capacity constraints on how many classes they can offer and age restrictions on when students can begin. This has led to spikes in demand for supplementary education offerings like our own Crimson Global Academy, one of the world's fastest growing accredited online high schools that helps ambitious students take extra A Levels or AP subjects alongside their traditional physical school.

One of the immediate problems you need to solve is that with the removal of the SAT Subject Tests, how will you convey to an admissions officer your competency in various academic subjects in a format they will readily understand. Instead of SAT Subject Test Chemistry, you can take AP Chemistry or A-Level Chemistry. Instead of SAT Subject Test Mathematics 2, you can take AP Calculus BC or A-Level Further Mathematics instead. The list goes on. There are plenty of viable alternatives to the subject tests. The key thing is that you are choosing a robust international curriculum that is widely understood and benchmarked so admissions officers don't have to guess at your ability level. Students from countries with weak national curriculum such as South Africa or New Zealand are going to be in a stronger position if they enroll in academic programs that let them take internationally recognized curriculum rather than their inferior local options.

Test-optional admissions is not terrifying. Let your competitors make the mistake of not taking the SAT or ACT while you continue to study hard and land useful scores. Find alternative ways to signal your academic ability now that the Subject Tests have been removed through Advanced Placement or A-Level examinations. Focus on finding ways to establish an audit trail for your entrepreneurial leadership projects and other extracurriculars so you can avoid the growing application fraud and build confidence in your admissions officer that you bring the goods.

The landscape is getting more competitive, but with these fundamentals in place, you can get ahead.

Chapter 10

Powerade, Burger Patties, and the Perfect Personal Statement

I have a magical connection to a chicken restaurant, head-quartered in Sydney, Australia, called Oporto.

Oporto is a fast food chain that sells a delicious, spicy burger called a Bondi Burger. When I was 15 years old, my best friend, Henry Chan, and I went to one of the local stores at our classic high school hang-out spot, Mission Bay. It was our first part-time job. We were going to do a three-day stint and learn the ropes. He was assigned to the front-of-house—taking customer orders, greeting people as they entered the fine establishment, and making sure they had a friendly experience. I was assigned to the deadly back-of-house role—it was my job to cook the burgers.

For me, Oporto was a kind of holy grail—an establishment that had delivered succulent chicken patties to me for years. The idea that I was going to be in charge of producing these fine, calorific specimens was crazy. In many ways, the experience was foundational.

Up until this point in my life, I'd never worked a part-time job. My family was not from a wealthy background, but my mother, Paula, had worked very hard building her company from scratch and had, in her own way, encouraged me to spend any extra time I had studying and focusing on reaching my academic goals. With that burning mission in mind, I had run hard at my academics at every stage. In the holidays, however, I enjoyed hanging out with my close friends and, for me, a couple of days at my favorite fast food restaurant sounded—well to be honest, like fun.

Up until this point in my life, I had also generally been able to do well at the one thing I was being judged on: school. As such, I hadn't experienced too many environments where I was a total disaster (well, except basketball, guitar, singing, soccer, rugby, and a long list of other activities at which I had tried and failed).

Oporto brought me a humbling wake-up call. At work, rather than being praised, I was being scolded for not folding the wrapping paper around each burger patty the right way (costing the franchise manager 2 cents with every piece of paper I had to throw in the trash!). Rather than being challenged and intellectually stimulated, I found myself standing in a stupor in between orders waiting for time to crawl by. Henry and I would come back from work and his parents wouldn't be able to stand in the same room as us from the grease smell that had soaked in our clothes. So basically, the realities of the working world hit me like a brick.

As I began to think about essay topics for my Common Application Personal Statement, the main essay that ends up getting sent to all US universities you apply to, I wracked my head for topics and my formative experience at Oporto jumped out. Yes, it was three days and so many braver teenagers than I had worked harder jobs for a lot longer periods of time. But in those three days, I had been exposed to an entirely new lens on life. My ego had been shattered as I realized that despite my apparent skill in mathematics and physics, that did not translate very well into being able to do the most basic kinds of wrapping or grilling.

A really good Common Application essay is one that exposes an entirely new side of you. It shows vulnerability, can be self-deprecating rather than flattering, highlights your creative writing ability, and may even make your admissions officer chuckle (after all, these people have to read hundreds if not thousands of essays over their time in the admissions office, so you might argue they deserve the odd laugh or two). So for me, the Oporto experience seemed to lend itself to all sorts of possibilities. Let me show you what I mean. Here was my essay:

The Surgeon

The apron drooped to my knees. I was emblazoned with the "'Hi, My Name is Jamie" sticker, coupled with a scarlet employee-in-training hat.

The "Fresh not Frozen, Grilled not Fried" motto resonated in my mind. It was July 2011. I had taken the plunge and secured my very first part-time job. I was flipping burgers, and I was excited.

I was accustomed to academia, to the sports field, to the stage, but this was an entirely fresh paradigm.

(continued)

(continued)

Anuj, the staff trainer and joyously friendly employee tasked with the rather unfortunate challenge of having to teach me hamburgerological cuisine, greeted me with a firm handshake. This guy meant business.

The familiar fast-food funk wafted through the tiny store like cologne in an airport duty-free store—overpowering, faintly nauseous, and all-encompassing.

The filing cabinets in my mind usually reserved for physics formulas, economics jargon, and debating cases were tipped out and crammed with permutations and combinations of burgers—Otropo, Chicken Wrappa, Bondi.

Exceptions to French conjugations were momentarily replaced with extra topping combos. The till became my new graphical calculator.

With surgeon-like precision Anuj modeled how to wrap a burger in four swift motions—place burger in the dead center, pull wrap from left to right, then right to left, then roll the corners.

He gestured toward his demonstration model and motioned for me to take to the stage. It was show time! Unfortunately, my burger ended up looking like the aftereffects of Hurricane Katrina. Anuj patted me on the back, said "you'll learn fast"—and smirked.

Suddenly the barricades were overrun and an influx of jandal-wearing, sun-glass-toting beach-goers charged into the store. The orders came flying faster than budget cuts at a Tea Party convention.

I heard the petrifying three words *chicken tenderloin combo*. This was it, the Everest of my culinary career.

It involved delving into the boss's prized stock of "succulent tenderloins" as he had described, "the highest quality meat we sell, expensive to buy and delicate to cook; we can't afford any mistakes." I was handling meaty gold.

As the first tenderloin slapped onto the grill with a satisfying sizzle, I could imagine the boss's scorching eyes scrutinizing my every action from behind the prying lens of the staff security camera.

Sun-glass toter number two, the tenderloin culprit, then muttered, "Excuse me! Sorry mate, my fault, I meant the chicken nuggets."

Silently, I screamed. I grimaced, pirouetted, and pleaded with the security camera.

Anuj saw my face, contorted in anguish, and took to the rescue with business-like efficiency. He rolled his eyeballs.

In one graceful movement he scooped the tenderloins and flicked them into the cooler with one hand, and in perfect synchrony, removed the emergency chicken nuggets with the other.

His eyes glistened with intensity. With consummate mastery his arms flicked from grill to cooker to table to bread to wrap. In less than 90 seconds, the order was complete. The boss's eyeballs returned to their sockets. The day was saved.

I worship the Anujs of this world. Certain jobs may look simple but that simplicity masks years of expertise. My skills in the rococo art of burger flipping paled into insignificance beside the master. I learnt more than burger flipping that day. I learnt humility, respect, and the value of a good chicken tenderloin.

What did you think?

Over the last eight years, I may have asked 500 different students this question from all over the world for interviews for our VIP program.

Generally, this is not what you expect for the magic required to land an offer at an esteemed institution like Harvard.

Quite to the contrary, I didn't realize it at the time but there is much to be taken from this essay about my sacred fast food restaurant, Oporto. I generally advise my students that the application essays can make up to as much as 20–30% of your candidacy for these top universities. In a sea of competition, where so many students have talented academic grades, interesting projects, and compelling references, a blank canvas in which you can show your authentic voice is one of the most powerful opportunities you have to grab the attention of admissions officers.

My application was filled with lists of Olympiad competitions, debate tournaments, Model UN conferences, additional A-Level subjects, passionate references, prefect roles, clubs I had created, and a wide range of other extracurriculars. My Oporto essay enabled me to showcase that I was more than happy to take a big fat laugh at myself and point out that although I may have a couple of strengths, I have a long list of weaknesses. I was willing to learn from Anuj (renamed to protect the hero's name from my story) and had deep respect for his mastery of the craft.

The essay also showcased one of my passions that was in some aspects of my application but wasn't a major theme—creative writing. I had packed my essay full of language techniques, so much so that it is hard to wade through a sentence without being whacked over the head by a metaphor, a simile, an alliteration, a hyperbole, or some other kind of device.

I had chosen to use decidedly colloquial language, something I use to this day, to showcase a bit of my "Kiwiana" or New Zealand heritage and add a bit of international flavor to what is an otherwise highly structured application process. It highlighted many of my passions: physics, debating, French, reading, and writing and perhaps also showed that I was willing to take some risks. A comedic essay that largely centered on the Marvel Avengers of fast food burger production, Anuj, was an unusual strategy.

So where do you need to start with your application essay? Over the years, I have seen a truly dizzying array of essays through Crimson Education and the answer to this question will often surprise you.

For one of our proud Harvard alumni and Y-Combinator graduate, the essay topic we went for was his experience playing cricket in his hometown village in India. The essay offered a unique perspective into the humility of his family's background, his burning passion for cricket, and the humbling friendships he had forged across socioeconomic and cultural boundaries through his beloved sport.

For one of our proud University of Pennsylvania alumni, the essay topic we chose was sitting on a bench in the Auckland central business district staring at the people wandering around and the fantastical, imaginary background stories he retrofitted to them on his artistic canvas.

For one of our proud Wharton alumni, her essay topic was about the student's father who had a freak, tragic ski accident and had almost entirely lost his memory. For a family that put so much focus on intellectual discussion and the growth of the mind, it was devastating. Fortunately, the father, through his resilience, support, and I'm sure some fantastic doctors, was able to regain his memory, but not before it thrust our student into one of the most challenging personal circumstances she had ever experienced.

I could go on but let's focus on you. What will you write about?

I recommend we start by imagining your life on a graph. On the y-axis, we plot emotional intensity and on the x-axis, we plot time. You want to go back all the way to your childhood and then imagine plotting all of your life's most defining moments. These can be intensively positive (high up on the positive end of the *y*-axis) or deeply negative (low down on the negative end of the *y*-axis). Go through and note the most extreme 15 moments—positive or negative. Write them in a list.

An extreme one for me, for example, was my 18th birthday in which I was able to change my last name officially to Beaton. My birth parents had gone through a divorce when I was young and for my whole life, I had carried the name of a man I had never met because changing it would require consent from both parents and I had never been in contact with one of them. I felt a great kind of catharsis when at 18 I was able to march into the passport registration office in the Auckland CBD and change my last name after years of having to explain awkwardly why the name all my friends called me, and I used at school, wasn't on my official documents.

So back to your 15 moments. Think about them and list them out. Don't be shy. Many of the things you write down you may never have actually vocalized or stated out loud. Think about deeply challenging personal circumstances, all the instances of adversity you have faced, times of extreme disappointment, times of shock and surprise, times in which you were thrust into unusual cultural environments, perhaps in different countries.

Sit there and really reflect. Most high schoolers run from moment to moment and never have an opportunity to really think about the most defining experiences of their life. What makes you tick? This is the ideal space you want to explore.

Feel free to ask your parents also—they may recall quite vividly moments that you have buried that are brilliant topics to explore. Generally, it is you, however, that thinks of the winning topic.

When it comes to my students, once they have their 15 concepts nailed, I usually encourage them to work hard to isolate their three most promising ideas. Essays that talk about when things were going to plan, or when you achieved what you were aiming for, are generally not winning essays. You usually want to zero in on the ideas that explore the most challenging moments of life as opposed to those that were most jubilant.

Next up, we move to the trashy first draft. The idea behind this is you sit down and just let your essay pour out. Don't worry about grammar, language techniques, or vocabulary. Just focus on getting the content out. What was the story? What was the environment? The people? The key images that you can vividly remember when you recount what happened? Drag out all the details you can.

If you think back to my Oporto essay, I made a big deal of a moment when a large crowd of people came into the store and I was panicked at the wave of orders I'd just received. I thought back to how I imagined that moment in my mind and the silent screaming that had ensued as I saw the cash register ringing up with orders. Find your special Oporto moment and build on the critical images to make the story leap off the page.

Remember the dynamics at play. Your admissions officer will often read your application essay in less than a minute. I advise my students to go deep on imagery, go deep on character, and make sure to use a thorough dose of self-deprecating humor where possible. Think about how much you read that goes in one ear and out the other. You need to grab the admissions officer's attention by an image so ridiculous, a plot twist so extreme, or an "in medias res" beginning that thrusts the reader right into the thick of the essay. With only 650 words, you don't have time to muck around.

Once you have your trashy first draft, think about it. I wrote three prospective Common Application essays. Alongside my essay about changing my last name, and

Life Support

I am a creature of peculiar habit. I am indifferent to black cats, falling mirrors, and Friday the 13th. But I do have one superstition, one cosmic fault that tastes like no other.

It was October 2011. Twenty-five examinations clogged my sclerotic examination schedule. For the past two weeks, I had habitually visited my local dairy. I would walk out with my voluminous plastic bag overbrimming with the awesome threesome—a twin-pack of Fry's Turkish Delight, two family packs of Kettle's Barbeque Chips, and two 750ml bottles of Blue Powerade. A cheery smile spread from ear to ear, and the rhythmic "have a good day" of Anuj, the dairy owner, bounced along behind me, synchronous to my step.

It was the morning of my economics exam. Scouring the chasms of the humming chiller at the back of the local dairy, my eyes sparkled with glee. Blue Powerades were in stock. Up on my tippy toes, I rather clumsily attempted to spring the magical juice out of its prison. One can clattered discordantly against the concrete floor. A disapproving grunt resonated from the counter. "Sorry mate!" I chimed, shoving the dairy owner's fallen angel back into its chilly bliss. Armed with my drink, I headed to the counter. Scanning the premises, looking sinister in my intensity, I finally spotted the buried treasure. The unmistakable purple hue of the Fry's Turkish Delight, cowering beneath the mainstream Dairy Milk and Mars bars, catalyzed a childish chuckle of content. My eyes finally detected the all-important crisp stand. Relaxed skimming quickly turned into a militarily efficient search-and-rescue operation. My pulse quickened. I couldn't find them.

"Don't worry, Jamie, I know you, my man. Saved the last packet for you!"

"Anuj, you're a good guy." My pounding heart slowly reclaimed its composure. No need for a defibrillator today.

The world's equilibrium was reestablished. I had the third panel in my triptych—Kettle's Barbeque Chips. My taste trifecta was complete.

For five years now without fail, Coca Cola, Fry's, and the Kettle Corporations' annual sales in the Otahuhu region have strangely correlated with my exam timetables. I can't rationalize my superstition. Amongst friends in our typical Kiwi laissez-faire nature, I am quite the logical character. Economics, mathematics, and physics have taught me much; cost-benefit analysis, game theory, trend projections. Debating has honed my powers of reasoning. I like decisions to be based on experiential research and logical thinking. I don't tend to hare off to the Tarot reader.

Those three absolutes represent an aberration to my otherwise axiomatic rule. You see, to me, the color of a black cat's fur is just a particular phenotypic expression. Breaking a mirror is just an expensive nuisance, not a seven-year curse. I am happy to fly on Friday the 13th. But for me, exam food is life support. The food's the thing. Just as Rafael Nadal kisses his locker before taking to center court, I bite a chunk out of my Turkish Delight, down a slug of my Powerade, and slip a chip (or eight) before setting off to the exam room.

I eagerly await the fresh challenge of college in America. Despite the prospect of sheep deprivation, I am mentally prepared to fly to foreign pastures, embrace opportunities, forge friendships, and craft a new lifestyle.

However, one question still stands.

Where am I going to find my Unholy Trinity in America?

my essay about working at Oporto, I also developed this draft (this was my final version not my trashy first draft to be clear).

Between the two drafts, one can see similarities in my use of language techniques, imagery and a recurring theme of teasing my oddities. I employed dialogue to give the admissions officer a sense of my relatively informal communication style to contrast to what one could imagine from my various involvements in writing, theatre, and literature. In both essays, I used academics as the backdrop for a lot of my comparisons—I am a nerd through and through, shown in the contrasts between this new realm of the burger shop against the backdrop of my academic experience and in the need for this bizarre pattern of snacks to support my packed exam schedule. I don't always recommend this, but my love of academics was perhaps too much a part of my personality, that neglecting to feature this would almost have seemed inauthentic to me.

Keep in mind that the Common Application in a given year offers up a really wide variety of differing questions as well as an open prompt. This effectively means you can write about literally anything you want. Although this is true, there are bad topics and avoiding bad topics is critical. Avoid cliches like the plague.

The admissions officer's email inbox is the zombie apocalypse of cliches. The same cliches arise from the dead on an annual basis to haunt their poor souls yet again, and they desperately have to clamber through the freaky realm searching for an escape path (the rare mind-blowing essay) like Dave Bautista in Army of the Dead.

Here are 10 of the classic bad topics choices you want to avoid:

1. Talking about a time you lost on the sports field in a major competition

2. Talking about moving to a new country as an immigrant when you were young and didn't speak English (although this is actually very challenging for someone to go through, the topic is so common that I haven't read a differentiated version of the essay yet in eight years)

3. Talking about how you want to make the world a better place in an abstract way (I believe you can solve some of the world's issues but a topic so ambitious that lacks specificity lacks credibility unless you have some unbelievable extracurricular achievements.)

4. Talking about the major science/mathematics competition you've been involved in (unless something makes you unique in this environment, such as one of my students who wrote an essay about being the only girl in the room in robotics competitions)

5. Talking about Model United Nations competitions or debate competitions and how it gave you a global perspective (I have read this many times and it generally struggles to find unique ground.)

6. Talking about the adversity that led up to your major achievement (You can lose the sincerity of the journey if your story ends up flaunting top achievements. Skip the major achievement entirely and focus on the grit of the journey.)

7. Talking about your future plans (Hypothesizing about the future in your essay is not as credible as analyzing some of your personal growth that has already happened. There are other types of essays that can be used to share future plans and aspirations. Focus on helping the admissions officer understand your distinctive character.)

8. Talking about the adversity that your grandparents went through and what you learned from it (Almost every time I read an essay about the adversity of grandparents, the child is often from a very successful family

in their current generation. This is often an inadvertent clue that the child had a relatively cushy childhood, which isn't necessarily bad but doesn't align with the message.)

9. Talking about that time you got a B in a class (This sends a clear signal that you haven't experienced much real adversity and are in your own palace in the clouds. I once had a student write an essay about failing mathematics in their second to last year and then what they did to rapidly upskill in the subject. Fun fact: he is now a Harvard graduate and yes, he did actually fail Year 12 mathematics!)

10. Talking about your experience doing anything that is illegal (Hopefully you haven't but generally best to be avoided—almost never a good idea. This is a higher education institution you are applying to after all!)

A final word of advice as you seek to find your winning essay topic.

All universities will tell you to "be yourself," "let your unique voice shine through," and other very soothing narratives. These same universities ruthlessly reject 90% of candidates without rhyme or reason or explanation. Don't trust the university. They aren't trying to help you get in. They are trying to get their best possible class admitted in an increasingly stressful academic environment without triggering unnecessary scrutiny as to the adverse consequences of a fairly brutal admissions process.

The result of "being yourself" is not necessarily always going to get you into a better, or your dream, university. If anything, this is the university tacitly telling you to "stay in your lane" so they can more easily estimate your level, ability, and contributions accurately and make their decisions accordingly. If you are a high-achieving, male, STEM applicant from Shanghai and you just love piano, violin, mathematics, and classical music, being yourself is a recipe for a painful admissions landscape. Universities systematically stack the odds against students with this type of profile because so many applicants apply with similar profiles. If you fit into a box like this, you need to actively find ways to differentiate.

The reality is, most of what we do as students in high school isn't particularly unique. The world is large enough that there are enough people with fairly similar backgrounds to you and me that it is highly unlikely that a meaningful amount of our experience isn't strikingly similar to other students. The unbelievable stories of incredibly unique applicants applying to college successfully are by definition unbelievable because they hardly ever exist.

I have sent almost 400 students to the Ivy League and for virtually all of them, we had to work hard during the essay development process to find differentiated unique topics often buried deep in the applicant's background. If your magic essay topic isn't obvious, don't worry, because it virtually never is. Good essays take a substantial amount of brainstorming.

The only recent example I can think of where the obvious essay jumped off the page was for one of our Te Ara A Kupe Beaton Scholars (a scholarship we started for indigenous New Zealand students[1]). This student had overcome substantial adversity to win a full scholarship to a local private school. She initially was given a 50% scholarship and her parents' reaction to the remaining tuition bill was "is that before or after the scholarship?"

She fortunately received a full scholarship and went on to be the first Maori head student of Saint Kentigern College. As she presented to an open day in her final year of the school, a young Samoan boy came up to her after she spoke, tugged on her top, and said "seeing you leading this role makes me feel as if this school is for me, too!" with earnest excitement. My student broke into tears realizing that much of the hardship, cultural discomfort, and apparently parallel universe she had seemed to live while being in this school filled with privilege was worth it because she was opening up the talent floodgates to more students from her own background. With each wave, the barrier lowered.

My point of differentiation was my first time working at a burger shop. I spent three days working there. I could easily have overlooked the moment and the experience, but as I dug through my emotional highs and lows and the moments that forced me to reexamine my environment and experiences, it stood out.

Good luck and get brainstorming!

Chapter 11

Dual Degrees and Why Double Dipping Opens Doors You May Not Know Existed

I am a huge fan of dual degrees. I try to take advantage of them at every opportunity.

A dual degree is a program in which you are able to effectively get two degrees for the price or time of one. In economics, there is a famous saying that there is "no such thing as a free lunch," but dual degrees are about as close as you can get in the realm of higher education.

I have seized this opportunity twice. First, at Harvard, I pursued an advanced standing program. This program lets you use existing high school qualifications (such as the A Levels in my case or the IB Diploma or the AP curriculum) to get college credits. In this case, my A Levels enabled me to get eight courses out of the 32 required courses at Harvard waived. For those who do this, you are given the option of graduating early or doing a master's degree in science (as I was studying applied mathematics).

Taking some challenging extra coursework sounded fun. When I first landed at Harvard, I jumped into Econ 1011a, known to be the most difficult undergraduate economics course. The p-sets (the Harvard term for "homework problems") would often create workings that went for literally pages as I waded through multivariable calculus and attempted to model abstract optimization problems under the guidance of the legendary Professor Edward Glaeser.

A fun fact about Professor Glaeser was that, when I was at Harvard he went on "The Today Show" to talk about his book *Triumph of the City*.[1] You know an urban economist has made it when he makes studying cities so cool that he sits in the same seat as pop stars like Miley Cyrus!

Alongside Econ 1011a, I took Stat 110 with Professor Joe Blitzstein. This was an "introduction to probability" but the term *introduction* was a bit of a euphemism. This was a heavy-duty course and it required me to work hard to wrap my head around a variety of different statistical distributions, their applications, and tackle the creative problems Joe would set in the tests.

Next up was Math 23a. This was my first pure mathematics course and involved mastering a significant number of proofs, which are a sequence of logic that rigorously validates various key principles in mathematics. The creativity behind the intellectual gymnastics to design them was fascinating, and half the time I wondered how anyone could have spotted some of these techniques. People would joke that applied mathematics is what you take at Harvard if you couldn't handle pure mathematics or physics. From my sample size of one, I'd be inclined to agree.

The final course in my freshman semester was the life-changing but bizarrely named CB23. Culture and Belief 23 turned out to be a seminar taught at Harvard Business School by two awesome Professors—Mihir Desai and David Ager. It was my first introduction to Harvard's famous case study method of analyzing businesses. It was also my first rigorous exposure to business strategy. Within a couple of lessons, I was sold. I wanted to master this world of entrepreneurship.

After taking what was considered to be a very difficult freshman semester, I figured, similar to high school, I could use a class spam strategy and take additional classes. I proceeded to take typically six classes/semester, which enabled me to finish five years of Harvard degrees in three years. In finance, a trade is called *pure arbitrage* when the trader makes a pure profit without taking any risk. Shaving off two whole years of time at university that I could use to build my career while taking challenging classes and getting two degrees for the price of one was my pure arbitrage.

The other dual degree I have taken so far is my Stanford MBA/MA in Education. In two years, I could have pursued only my MBA but instead, I was able to use some of my electives to take various courses at the Stanford Graduate School of Education. Same formula: two years, two degrees rather than one. I wouldn't do this if the second degree was in a field I didn't have passion for, but I loved education so I considered this a no-brainer.

Now, as a prospective college applicant, you need to make sure you are aware of some of the most compelling dual degree opportunities available. Basically, there are three different types:

1. Combined bachelor's and master's degree programs in the same field (often requiring challenging graduate-level coursework)
2. Combined bachelor's and master's degree programs in differing fields
3. Two bachelor's degrees in the time that one would usually take

I generally prefer opportunities to get a master's degree and a bachelor's degree over two undergraduate degrees, but you won't always have the option.

Here is a summary of ten of the most compelling dual degrees in the US you should be thinking about.

THE HUNTSMAN PROGRAM AT THE UNIVERSITY OF PENNSYLVANIA[2]

I love the University of Pennsylvania because it is home to Wharton, which is generally regarded to be the world's best undergraduate business school. Wharton is like a Wall Street assembly line. It trains you in financial modeling, strategy, marketing, leadership, human resources, and many other areas. My Harvard classmates used to be a bit nervous in job interviews when Wharton kids turned up because they always have such extensive training, whereas liberal arts degree students are often relying on the training programs of Wall Street banks or management consulting firms to get them up to speed.

Back in high school, I was delighted to find the Huntsman Program. It is a unique dual degree that takes only 50 students each year from around the world. Students receive a bachelor of arts with a major in international studies and a Wharton business degree (a bachelor of science because Wharton has turned the art of business into a science apparently). Students are also expected to choose a target language. I chose French when I applied. In this target language, the student will take advanced language skills and even do an exchange program. The program strives to recruit international students and to create a class that is very international in its composition.

The Huntsman Program is the perfect program for talented Model United Nations diplomats to apply for, thinking they want to end up at the United Nations before realizing that nothing much happens there and then switching to work on Wall Street. I am joking, of course, but in all seriousness, there are few programs in the world that are so effective at placing their alumni into the most competitive jobs in investment banking, private equity, and management consulting.

I was so compelled by this program and they did such a good job selling it during the preview days, I almost went to the Huntsman program over Harvard. Almost. Crimson has sent close to 10 students to Huntsman over the last several years, which is quite a feat given they only take 50 a year (and usually only 15 are international students).

JEROME FISHER MANAGEMENT AND TECHNOLOGY AT THE UNIVERSITY OF PENNSYLVANIA[3]

University of Pennsylvania is not home to one but two of my favorite dual degrees. Jerome Fisher, although it is often considered to be the slightly less exclusive cousin of the Huntsman Program, may just be the most employable program around. Graduates receive a bachelor of science in an engineering field as well as a bachelor of science from Wharton Business School. The most in-demand skills in the world today are data science, statistics, engineering, mathematical modeling, finance, and business. Jerome Fisher equips you with all of these skills. Although UPenn is no MIT when it comes to engineering, I would personally rather have the incredible finance training ground of Wharton, and a slightly weaker engineering program, than the reverse. This program is well worth your consideration.

BROWN–RHODE ISLAND SCHOOL OF DESIGN DUAL DEGREE[4]

I am a practical fellow and like to guide my students toward degrees that have very clear job opportunities. As such, I generally get a little squeamish when I have a student who is considering a pure music or pure art program. I am all for following passions, but it is so unbelievably hard to make a career in these fields that I would rather my students make their academic training in an area that is slightly more versatile and broadly applicable.

That said, Rhode Island School of Design (RISD) is the Wharton of arty programs. It is often regarded as the best undergraduate architecture and product design school in the world. I recently was training a student of mine from New Zealand who was the student body president of RISD and was interviewing for Harvard Business School's 2+2 program. What kind of architect wants to do an MBA? An architect who wants to run the show.

Brown, as you know, is an Ivy League school and this dual degree combines two bachelor's degrees from RISD and from Brown. At Brown, you can take coursework in areas such as computer science or economics or even go wild and embrace some intellectually luxurious coursework in litera-ture, art history, or other such fields. As a passionate wan-nabe English major myself, I couldn't quite pull the trigger on an English major because I am a bit too career focused and joke to my students that such coursework is "luxurious" because if you were starving and needed your degree to pay for itself, English wouldn't be your first or your seventh bet.

But I like this dual degree because it gives you all the em-ployability of a traditional Ivy League undergraduate degree but it also lets you still follow your passion for art if you are so inclined. Unfortunately, I am quite lacking in this area so this wasn't an option on my table, but I hope you are an aspiring da Vinci and can achieve things that were beyond me!

UNIVERSITY OF CALIFORNIA BERKELEY'S MANAGEMENT, ENTREPRENEURSHIP AND TECHNOLOGY PROGRAM[5]

This program appears to be the Jerome Fisher program from Wharton transplanted and dropped on the West Coast so you can avoid the painful East Coast winters while still being employable anywhere. The program gives you two bachelor of science degrees. It is highly selective and applicants need to apply directly for the program; they can't easily transfer into the program after getting into another school at UC Berkeley.

I really like this program because of its location—Silicon Valley. Combining a strong business program with incredibly useful STEM majors such as industrial engineering and operations research and throwing you into the best job market in the world is a winning equation. This program will be hard work. Engineering at UC Berkeley is notoriously challenging. But, on the other side of all that pain will be some glorious opportunities.

HARVARD–NEW ENGLAND CONSERVATORY[6]

I consider this to be one of the great masterpieces for aspiring musicians. The career pathway for someone doing pure music, even if they go to Juilliard, is quite simply challenging. You are often having to work side gigs for many years to fund your lifestyle as you try and make it big as a performer. Even "making it big" and landing prestigious positions in certain orchestras or music groups may still not easily cover the bills. For some, that pathway is their dream. For those who are more practically inclined (and willing to work extremely hard in high school) comes the glorious Harvard–NEC dual degree program.

Our very own vice president of product at Crimson, as I write this, is a graduate of this program. Graduates receive a bachelor of arts from Harvard as well as master's in music from the New England Conservatory. This is a wonderful way to chase your music performance ambitions alongside one of the best human capital insurance policies—a Harvard undergrad degree.

COLUMBIA–JUILLIARD[7]

This program is perhaps even stronger than Harvard–NEC. For one, Juilliard is the mecca of music programs, and usually, consistently, tops the dream school list for my aspiring music and theatre students around the world. Additionally, the location of New York is one of the best places to be, given the thriving music scene and some of the best museums in the world. Finally, Columbia has a very strong foundation in the humanities given its core curriculum and stronger orientation in these areas than perhaps even Harvard.

One of my recent students was admitted into Columbia–Juilliard. At the age of 14, she got a Violin Licentiate Diploma. When she went to New York for her audition, a violin shop owner was so impressed by her ability, he lent her a $US100 thousand violin for several months for her high-stakes audition. She is loving the program.

STANFORD COTERMINAL MASTER'S PROGRAM[8]

A number of my most talented students who have gone to Stanford have taken the Coterminal Master's Program. As the name suggests, this lets you complete a master's degree alongside your undergraduate degree. This is the Stanford equivalent of the Harvard advanced standing program I did myself. It is not an easy pathway and often requires quite a number of challenging graduate-level courses, but I've heard rave reviews and most of my highly academic STEM students at Stanford in recent years have pursued this program.

I think this is particularly valuable for those studying computer science. One of my students in the coterm program recently had his Harvard Business School 2+2 interview as well before heading off to be a product manager at Uber. In his master's program, he took machine learning, deep learning, artificial intelligence, natural language processing, convolution neural networks, systems, and algorithms.

I challenge you to design a more employable set of courses than that!

3 + 2 ENGINEERING PROGRAMS[9]

One of the smoothest pathways into an Ivy League school such as Columbia is the 3 + 2 program. Getting into an Ivy League school directly like Columbia University is exceptionally difficult, especially for STEM majors who face so much competition. 3 + 2 engineering programs combine three years at a variety of liberal arts colleges followed by two years of engineering at an engineering school (such as Columbia) and typically result in you graduating with a bachelor of arts from the liberal arts program and a bachelor's in engineering from the engineering school.

There is substantial opportunity for candidacy arbitrage here, that is, a candidate who wouldn't usually be able to get into Columbia University going through one of the liberal arts program feeders and finally graduating with a dual degree (and an Ivy League undergrad engineering degree at that).

One of my students did this very successfully. He began his undergrad degree at Carleton College where he played varsity tennis. After strong performance in his undergraduate degree, he was able to transfer into Columbia University where he completed a bachelor of science in operations research. This student has gone on to work at high-growth technology company, Didi (the Uber of China), and now works in investment banking.

I personally would love the academic combination of an immersive undergraduate liberal arts education coupled with two intensive years of engineering. It is important to understand which of the 3 + 2 programs have guaranteed relationships between the liberal arts college and the engineering college and which have applications or other entrance criteria. Conditional on doing your homework, this is an exciting option.

VAGELOS LIFE SCIENCES AND MANAGEMENT AT THE UNIVERSITY OF PENNSYLVANIA[10]

Yes, my love affair for the University of Pennsylvania continues. This is because the pairing of interesting degrees with the highly employable Wharton undergraduate degree makes for a lot of fascinating options. The LSM Program combines a Wharton undergraduate degree with a bachelor of arts in a life science area.

Typically, students who find this to be exciting were previously considering medicine but then discovered they had an interest in business and entrepreneurship. This program is wonderful if you are fascinated by topics such as drug development and commercialization, biomedical device development, or the "business" of science. The program encourages its graduates to go into the "financial and strategic management of life science organizations."

One of my students who has now graduated from the program completed his Wharton degree with dual majors in statistics and finance and his bachelor of arts in neuroscience. He has gone on to found his own organization immediately after graduating. When I first met him, he was having second thoughts on becoming a doctor, and through the LSM Program he has carved out his distinctive career path in the science field.

DIGITAL MEDIA DESIGN AT THE UNIVERSITY OF PENNSYLVANIA[11]

At this point, I should disclose that I am not being sponsored by UPenn! I do have great respect for how they curate very thoughtful degree combinations that provide graduates a very explicit set of skills that can help them thrive in the job market. This theme continues with DMD, or Digital Media Design.

This program is a bit of an exception to the rule on this list because it is interdisciplinary but doesn't actually result in two degrees. I thought it was still worth the inclusion, however, as it is a golden example of some of the gems out there that you might never have heard about. I know a lot of students who would not usually consider taking the risk of pursuing a career in animation and design, but through a program like this, they are willing to take the plunge.

Students receive a bachelor's in engineering and science, which combines coursework from computer graphics, communication theory, and fine art courses. The program was launched in response to an open opportunity to train more graduates for an opening in the expanding computer graphics and animation industry.

One of my students who went to DMD was strong in high school in mathematics and physics but had a burning passion for fine arts. He loved drawing photos of transformers, sci-fi characters and his own reincarnations of illustrations from anime and video games. When we came across DMD, we knew we had found a powerful fit!

So what is my final word on dual degrees?

The fact is, you are going to spend usually four (or at a sprint three years) in your undergraduate degree, so you want to do the critical research to make sure you aren't overlooking a relevant, niche program. Many of the students I have sent to the aforementioned dual degrees had never heard of them before, but they quickly fell in love after being exposed to them.

Although reputations are important, and I don't encourage my students to compromise, sometimes through dual degrees you can have it all and combine a highly employable degree alongside one of your passion fields and potentially open up a unique set of career opportunities (while keeping other more mainstream doors open!).

Chapter 12

What the Rich Get Wrong

Don't Pay to Play over Summer

When I was in high school, I had never heard of the "summer program." I received my education on the US teenage culture through the astute tutelage of the American Pie series. From the notorious band camp in *American Pie* to the more general summer camps that served as the setting of many horror movies that my friends and I used to watch voraciously in high school, the idea of hanging out with a lot of friends in a remote location sounds like a blast. The concept didn't really exist in New Zealand. Most people would spend a week or so with their friends at a music festival or at the beach getting too much sun, but there were limited structured programs. This is partially a symptom of the lack of a comprehensive college admissions program outside of the US.

US universities definitely incentivize the creation of massive summer programs in order to fulfill supplemental essay questions like Stanford's notorious "What did you do over the last two summers?" You can't quite answer that by saying you drank Mountain Dew and played Call of Duty. As US colleges have become the most popular destination for the world's most ambitious young people, US summer programs have become increasingly global. More generally, the idea of using your holidays to proactively build your résumé has also spread.

In my time in high school, I used my breaks to complete multiple hiking expeditions for my Duke of Edinburgh Gold Award, went to an international Model United Nations conference (where I met my Crimson cofounder, Sharndre), attended the Rotary Science and Technology Forum (which ironically persuaded me that I did not want to pursue science at university), participated in tennis programs, studied for various extra subjects outside of school, and prepared for various standardized tests. I also spent time with my friends and took some important leisure time out from the crazy marathon of hustle that is high school (when your aspiration is an Ivy League acceptance!).

Over the last eight years, we have helped guide thousands of our students through the strategic question of how to plan out your summers and what to do to get the most out of them. Let me share some of the key learnings.

First, avoid "paying to play" over summer. There is a huge industry of summer programs that can cost anywhere from $US3,000 to $US10,000+. Some of these programs are useful. The majority are a total and absolute waste of time.

I remember one day when I got home from school, I had received some information in the mail from an amazing sounding event called the "Global Young Leaders Conference (GYLC)." Wow, I thought to myself. What an opportunity! Some smart person in the US has managed to find out that I may have some awesome potential and has invited me to their exclusive conference.

Wrong.

This organization is a classic example of a disastrous use of time and money over the summer. Organizations such as GYLC are for-profit and typically buy your information from testing organizations such as the SAT and ACT. As a result, like clockwork, your mailbox begins to get filled with prestigious sounding opportunities and invitations for these exclusive competitions. They talk of application deadlines, the need to apply early, and the results of their graduates.

I almost got sucked in. Several times in fact. The first was when I thought getting an invitation to GYLC made me special and would add something to my application. The second was when I got invited to join a National Honor Society of sorts that involved paying to sign up and register to receive my award (that I hadn't applied for).

I really despise these types of organizations that insert themselves into the already chaotic world of college admissions and lure ambitious young candidates in by shadowing many of the characteristics of what a top university might look like: exclusive, competitive, ambitious.

One of the ways to detect if a program is a waste of time is to ask if it is actually selective. Typically, programs such as GYLC will accept materially all the students who apply that meet basic conditions. As long as you can pay their fee, they will generally accept you.

This is a bad sign. We learned this back in my introduction when I introduced Gary Becker's famous economic signaling. If you go to these programs, you hurt yourself.

First, you could be going to a more selective program that is academically challenging and actually means something to prospective universities because you had to be of a certain level to qualify. Second the fact that you attended this program (and paid for it) suggests either you are a little naive or that you were unable to secure a more solid opportunity for the summer.

The second way to detect whether or not a program is a waste of time is to carefully study the itinerary. When I got off my initial wave of excitement and really studied the GYLC itinerary, I realized just how much sight-seeing and general tourist activities were incorporated. This didn't seem like some kind of elite academic experience but rather a kind of family holiday to stroll past the White House. There is a time and place for everything, and generally pay-to-play programs like GYLC are not the best way to discover the nuances of the US's history and landmarks.

Second, when possible, focus on applying for high-caliber programs that are *directly* affiliated with legitimate universities.

For example, just because a program uses the word *Oxbridge* doesn't mean it is a bona fide Oxford- or Cambridge-affiliated opportunity. I know this because the sprawling array of "Oxbridge Summer Programs" was another trap I nearly fell for in high school.

What could be a better way to show my passion for getting into Oxford or Cambridge than attending one of their summer programs! The reality is these programs actually have nothing to do with Oxford or Cambridge. They simply pay rental fees to various universities like Oxford or Cambridge to be able to appear to have some kind of formal relationship. They may even employ current students of the programs to teach various courses. Don't be fooled, however; these programs are, at best, well-meaning academic excursions that take virtually everyone that applies and, at worst, the charlatans of college admissions.

Even if you are going to apply for an unselective summer program, it is better to pursue such a program with a directly affiliated university partner. A good example of this is the Harvard Summer Program for High School Students.[1] Harvard's Summer Program basically takes everyone who applies. In all my years at Crimson, I can't recall anyone who has been rejected from this program. I'd like to believe all my Crimson kids are the rock stars of high school students globally (and although this is pretty accurate most of the time), not all of them are. Chances are if my students have never been rejected, the program is basically unselective.

Even though getting into Harvard's program isn't necessarily sending a signal that you passed some selective door, the program is high caliber and you receive real college credit. Many of the courses taken are real university courses offered by Harvard undergraduates, so the experience is a fairly authentic representation of aspects of the student experience.

A good idea is to take courses in areas your school doesn't usually offer. In high school, I was passionate about economics and wanted to learn more about investing but there was little in the way of formal coursework I could explore. A great choice would have been the Harvard Secondary School Program's "Introduction to Capital Markets and Investments." This would show a prospective admissions officer that I have gone beyond the general bounds of a high school economics curriculum and was already exploring relevant skills to finance. This is one of the important ways in which you can use unselective summer programs: to show "intellectual vitality."

Stanford defines "intellectual vitality" as "a commitment, dedication and genuine interest in expanding your intellectual horizons. . . . We want to see the initiative with which you seek out opportunities and expand your perspective." In other words, you aren't getting into Stanford just by mastering your high school coursework. Consider using your summer to address this aspect of the Stanford criteria.

Third, the holy grail if you can achieve it is getting into the highly competitive summer programs. I already told you about MIT's RSI Institute. Other notable programs include the Stanford University Mathematics Camp (SUMaC).[2] There are only two options one can pursue at SUMaC. First, Abstract Algebra and Number Theory. Second, Algebraic Topology. These are both topics I didn't explore until studying applied mathematics at Harvard—and I considered myself a good mathematics student. You get the idea: not anyone who enjoys a bit of calculus can waltz into this program. Getting in sends a clear signal to the admissions committee of top colleges that you are talented in mathematics. One of my recent admits to Harvard, for example, did SUMaC as one of his major summer activities in his final summer prior to the application.

Another example is Yale's Young Global Scholars program (YYGS).[3] This one has a meaty application process which in some ways mimics the Common Application itself. YYGS even lets you apply to an area of study that is of particular interest to you, such as politics, law and economics (PLE) or innovations in science and technology (IST). It's also pretty selective, so another great one to send the right signals to admissions officers reading your summer resume.

A final example is the Summer Science Program.[4] This is an independent charitable program that has run for six decades (yes, a 60-year-old summer program!). You can often tell a great summer program by the humility of the website. The best programs typically have the most nondescript websites. Some of the worst programs often have the most flashy, marketing hype. One of my talented aspiring scientists was recently admitted into SSP. Here is what her acceptance email wrote:

Congratulations! The SSP Admissions Committee has accepted your application to the Summer Science Program in Biochemistry.

This year we received 1,800 applications from outstanding students around the world for only 180 spots—108 in Astrophysics and 72 in Biochemistry—so you can be sure that your colleagues will be just as bright and interesting as you are. The opportunity to collaborate with them on research will be unforgettable and exhilarating

Simple, elegant yet incredibly effective. This program has an acceptance rate of 10%! Never mind their fairly outdated website, getting into SSP means business. The program was originally founded as a collaboration between the California Institute of Technology and The Thacher School (a private school in California), but it has become a juggernaut of its own.

Fourth, you don't necessarily have to go to a competitive summer program. Some of the best summer itineraries I have worked with my students to design don't involve any of the structured programs. A good summer definitely needs to be structured, but if you are self-motivated with some clear discipline, you can have a very productive summer without going to any of these programs.

Some of my students have led fascinating social initiatives over the summer. I think about one of my students who partnered with a number of local cafes and collected their excess fruit. She would turn these into smoothies and arrange to hand them out to the homeless community. After taking an interest in dentistry, she had learned that sometimes it was challenging to supply the right nutrients to this community because of the decay of the teeth in some of these individuals which meant eating hard fruits (like apples) were actually quite painful. A smoothie was a fairly low-risk way to ensure strong fruit dosages.

Other students have used time over the summer to prepare for competitive science fair competitions, Olympiads, or upcoming performances. Some have used the time to learn a new language or work on a mobile application. You can stay in your home country and for very little cost learn immersively on platforms such as Coursera, taking high-caliber courses from leading universities. Some of my favorites are Yale's "Introduction to Psychology," Wharton's "Business and Financial Modeling Specialization," and Harvard's CS50 program. These are all low-cost online programs that offer compelling material that can expose you to concepts you are unlikely to see in a traditional high school education.

Fifth, get a job! Getting real work experience in a fast-food chain such as a McDonalds or a KFC will teach you some very powerful life lessons. Many students have no choice but to work over the summer, because they need to support their family. A clear sign of privilege in the application process is when a student has never worked any job throughout high school (somewhat embarrassing me before my Oporto's experience).

Although there is nothing necessarily wrong with never having had a part-time job, there is a lot to be said for someone who is firmly grounded in the realities of the working world and knows what it is like to come home, exhausted, after standing up for eight hours serving customers. Beyond the real-world lessons, this can be a useful differentiator on your Common Application because I don't see many applicants to the top US universities with this kind of part-time job.

Another type of experience worth considering is a virtual internship (or an in-person one if possible). One of my recent admits to Stanford had the fortunate opportunity to intern for a local investment management firm in his home country. He was looking to gain exposure to investing, and this was a brilliant way to more concretely explore his interests. Internships are a great way to sense check the theoretical career ambitions you may hold and potentially rule out pathways that are definitely not for you.

When I was younger, I thought I wanted to do medicine (for all the wrong reasons). It wasn't until I began seriously looking into the experience of working in a hospital that I realized this wasn't for me. To my naive high school understanding, doctors had a highly structured working environment spending almost their entire work inside the white walls of the hospital dealing with people in generally distressing conditions. Although I liked science in theory, the practical job dynamics, repetitive nature of the work, and impact model of working patient by patient (constraining your impact to a function of how many hours you put in) didn't suit my particular personality.

Often you will be able to cold-email local firms and procure unpaid (if you are able to do this) work experiences. Even a couple of days at a firm can give you an eye-opening perspective on an entire industry.

Recently, one of my MBA students who studies at Johns Hopkins University thought she was interested in the fashion industry. She did a number of discovery calls into what it was like working at *Vogue*, her childhood dream. She quickly realized that this was an industry in secular decline where most interns could go unpaid for several years and many digital content producers have to cover celebrity news wall-to-wall to generate clicks to eke out advertising dollars and impressions. The glitz and glamor of Anna Wintour and *The Devil Wears Prada*, and the humble realities of the secular decline of the traditional print magazine, couldn't be more antithetical. A couple of conversions or a few days spent working in your target industry can refine your thinking, which might hang around for years if unexplored.

A final experience worth considering is doing research over the summer. If you have a strong academic background in any discipline, chances are you can get an early jump into academia and find a budding PhD student or professor who may have a project you can assist with (at Crimson we have a program called Crimson Research Institute, which teams our students with college professors or PhDs for that very purpose). Consider no work to be beneath you as you seek to hoover up knowledge about how the world of research works!

If you do a good job, you will often be given increasing levels of responsibility because many research teams are perpetually underfunded. If possible, try and participate in projects that end up getting published where you can be a coauthor. This gives you a concrete achievement that can be highlighted to colleges. Even if you don't get published, time spent working on research topics will often show the valuable "intellectual vitality" criteria in spades for an admissions committee assessing your case.

Over the summer, you can also get your academics cranking. Get your standardized prep work under control. If you can cram for the SAT and get those assessments out of the way in a highly productive sprint, you can avoid it hanging over your head during the school year when you are trying to steer your GPA to the skies. It is also a great time to study for additional Advanced Placement subjects or other formal qualifications. It can be hard to find the headspace for entirely new subjects when you are in the throes of a difficult semester, but the summer will often give you the space you need to conquer some new intellectual pursuits!

Whatever you do, make sure your summer is structured, so when you are writing your Stanford supplement in the future and answering "How did you spend your last two summers?" you have something meaningful to show for it! Be careful not to fall for the glossy material in the mail. An authentic set of academically enriching activities over the summer coupled with some quality family time can often be a great recipe for success as long as you are pushing yourself and making tangible progress.

Chapter 13

Why Student Athletes Need to Compete with Their Heads

One of the truly unique aspects of the US college admissions process that I found bizarre as an international student is athletic recruitment. What if I told you that if you had a certain kind of superpower a college like Harvard might actually change all of its rules for you? Hard to believe? Athletics is that superpower.

The Ivy League after all is not an academic union but rather was an athletic affiliation among eight universities. It just so happened that these eight schools had some of the strongest academic achievements around. Over time, the affiliation between the Ivy League and athletics started to wane and in popular culture *Ivy League* generally refers to the academic powerhouse of academic powerhouses of global universities.

At each of the top universities, a substantial portion of incoming slots are generally filled by athletes. Harvard, for example, has 41 Division 1 sports teams.[1] Division 1 is the highest tier of competitive athletics. Each of these teams need to be filled with brilliant talent. As a result, a full 20% of incoming freshman at Harvard are generally recruited athletes for whom a significant portion of why they are admitted is not their academic abilities but rather their athletic talent.

When I was at Harvard, I had a quick introduction to the world of athletics. The class was "Introduction to Nutrition and Global Health." As an eager freshman, I did my pre-reading and would answer the questions of the professor as regularly as I could contribute. One day the professor announced there would be a group project and we were to form a group. I didn't really know anyone in this class but before I could think too deeply about my problematic social situation, two people popped up next to me. The first thing I noticed was that these two guys were very tall. I am pretty short myself and generally am used to most people being taller than I am. In order for someone to really grab my attention, they have to be really tall. These guys if you don't get the idea already were very, very tall.

"Jamie (they knew my name?), would you like to be in our group project team?" Friendly and naive, I was a bit flattered these two had approached me so quickly. "Sure," I remarked. As the group project began to kick into action, I would send emails to my two classmates seeing if they wanted to catch up to begin work. No response. I would ask these two in class if they had seen my emails and if they wanted to catch up. "Sure, let's do it." I'd leave class and then send an email. No response.

This seemed peculiar to me. Maybe they didn't check their emails? Time wore on and gradually it dawned on me. Maybe these two students didn't really intend on doing all that much in this group project. I don't know whether it was my eager enthusiasm to answer questions or my taste in Abercrombie and Fitch jackets 10 years after they were cool that attracted these guys to me. It was probably the fashion sense.

Fast-forward to the last couple of days before the final presentation. I had learned something interesting about these two. One was a freshman recruit for Harvard's football team. The other was a graduating senior who was Harvard's most famous basketball player of many years. He was soon heading to NBA try-outs in Las Vegas. I received a text from the rising NBA all-star. "Jamie, I have try-outs this week in Las Vegas. I am going to be flying down and will only be flying back the morning of our presentation. Would you be able to help me out?"

At least, he had the courtesy of dropping me a text.

The last time I had hauled my entire team through a group project was in Year 5 when I made our group's Japanese tourism advertising flier for social studies class and my teammates didn't do anything. I was at Harvard but apparently I had not yet quite escaped the hot mess that is the group project.

I cared about getting As and didn't want to mess up my GPA in this class so I gritted my teeth, laughed a little, and got to work. I made the entire presentation. Then I realized that even though I had made the whole presentation, when my classmates decided to grace our nutrition class, they would have no idea what to present on. Checking the rubric, I realized "participation" was awarded for sharing the responsibilities around the group during the final presentation. I face palmed and resorted to the secret weapon of every primary school speech competition—cue cards.

Here, I was a Harvard freshman. I had seemingly conquered the juggernaut of high school to land a place at this esteemed university. Well past midnight, I had finished making cue cards for my football and basketball teammates. I figured out how to print these cue cards.

The next morning without missing a beat, Mr. NBA all-star rolled into class. I looked at him frankly impressed by how evidently well practiced he was at running this group project ruse. "Please read these cue cards. All you have to do is read the cue cards."

Our group presented and as we delivered our (my) project, I had to give it to these guys. They knew how to wing a presentation. They read my cue cards with consummate mastery. The class applauded. I got my A.

I learned a valuable lesson about athletic recruitment at Harvard.

I didn't miss a beat. I generally advise against making the same mistake twice. From then on, I assembled crack teams of super academic students for all group projects. My crew: Lillian, David, Sami, and Devret, who have gone on to work at Bain, Goldman Sachs, LinkedIn, and Google, respectively. They were the Green Berets of group projects. The team had strong computer science, statistical analysis, financial analysis, and strategy skills. We knocked projects out of the park often scoring on the highest scale of 90%. From then on, I never jumped into group projects with strangers again. I realized at Harvard that the top students didn't even wait to form group projects once class had begun. They would take classes already knowing who their A-scoring group project squad was going to be. I followed suit and didn't look back.

In all seriousness, there are many incredibly talented athletes at these great universities. They do an amazing job of balancing 20 hour/week+ training schedules with athletics. Many of the most hard-working, disciplined people I knew at Harvard came from an athletic background.

With that necessary disclaimer out of the way, let's talk about athletic admissions.

College coaches, as we saw in the Varsity Blues Scandal, have a large influence on who gets accepted into top universities. Once a coach has decided they want to recruit a certain student for their team, they give the green light to admissions and it dramatically boosts that student's odds of being accepted. College coaches are primarily incentivized by their sports team performing. These are competitive people who are trying to recruit top athletes, not top academics. If this system was left unchecked there would be a gaping divide between the academic scores of those admitted for their academics and those admitted for their athletics.

In order to combat this problem, the Ivy League and many other highly ranked US universities give their coaches rules for the academic criteria underpinning whom they can admit. Generally, at Harvard, the rule of thumb is the average SAT score of recruited athletes for a Harvard sports team must fall within one standard deviation of the mean SAT score of Harvard students. This places a bound on the athletic recruitment because if the coach tries to take too many athletes with weak academic profiles, the SAT score average of the team will fall outside of acceptable bounds and the admissions office is likely to intervene.

It is worth noting that many of these academic guidelines only limit the average SAT score in the team, which means that on the extremes, big exceptions can be made for talent. At Harvard, I met a talented squash player who was the US national champion. She briefly mentored in Crimson's athletic department but her unbelievable success in sport made that short-lived. When Harvard recruited her, they knew this girl was going places. As a result, they were willing to give her some flexibility on her SAT score. She was admitted with an SAT score that was basically the US national average score. Typically, at Harvard, most applicants are scoring in the 95th to 99th percentile. This is an extreme example because few athletes go on to be national champions but it does show that if you are actually at the top of your country in a sport, these great institutions are willing to bend their criteria.

So what sort of athlete should you be besides one that's good enough at their sport to get recruited. And the answer is—especially if you're looking at the Ivies—not necessarily the best on the team. The ideal profile for admission to the Ivy League when it comes to athletics is generally not someone who is at the top at their athletic game but very weak in their academics. The winning profile is actually the athlete who can offset the weak academics of other student athletes who take to the podium each year.

As long as you are sufficiently good to be playing for one of these college's top sports teams—even on the bench—you want to boost your academics as much as possible. This flips the equation above on its head. Rather than being an academic tax for the recruitment coach, your existence lets them go and find one of the athletes they really want—a super high-performing athlete with weaker academics. Of course, in a magical world you can have leading academics and athletics, but usually the time trade-off that these pursuits require necessitates that sacrifices are made. In general, it is better to be a high-performing athlete with brilliant academics than a strong athlete with weak academics. You will have far more options.[2]

Many high school athletes have so much of their identity tied up in their sporting success because they are walking superheroes in their school communities that they start overlooking their academics. They don't study much for the SAT. They let their GPA slide. When it comes to applying to college, they haven't taken much in the way of extension coursework. This is not the winning strategy.

The winning strategy as an athlete is to compete with your head. You don't need to beat super nerd academic students. You do need to beat 95%+ of athletes at the academic game. This generally shouldn't be too difficult because many aren't playing the academic game. Many athletes are pumping their efforts into sports. If you embark on some focused SAT tutoring, are disciplined about your high school GPA, and make sure you don't miss critical exams and shoot yourself in the foot, you will quickly carve out a big advantage over other applicants.

This is also generally a much more effective career strategy. It is very hard to make it as a professional athlete. If you bet all your eggs on sports and you are in the significant majority who can't crack it at the big leagues, you are often left in a challenging career position. Our Crimson advisory board member and Olympic Gold Medalist Barbara Kendall joined us because she is so passionate about making sure that athletes get their education and have that back-up for later in life.

If you pursue the strategy of getting your sports to a competitive level but still compete with your head, you can get into a top university and then be seriously desirable in the job market. At my old hedge fund Tiger, one of the most historically successful Wall Street firms of all time, Julian Robertson, was notorious for loving to recruit college athletes. They were fantastically competitive, disciplined, and willing to work hard. I remember starting at Tiger and meeting my colleague Nate. He was a Rhodes Scholar, a National Football champion, and I think you could literally stack two of me side by side and I would struggle to get to his wing length from shoulder to shoulder.

Wall Street figured out early that athletes have many of the most powerful traits that make for highly effective workers and leaders. The problem is if you don't invest in your academics, you'll never make the cut to get into the right tier of university that then unlocks these awesome job opportunities.

The exact balance is delicate. You need to know what the minimum thresholds are at all your target universities for a sports recruit and then optimize your time allocation between academics and athletics accordingly. Many of my students don't have the sporting acumen to be able to pull this off, but if you are in the minority that do possess some strong sporting ability, I highly encourage you to go for the recruited athlete pass. It is one of the most reliable channels into one of the world's best US universities.

It is worth noting that the US is the only major country that has this exception channel for athletes. Oxford, Cambridge, and the rest of the UK universities have strict academic criteria and generally consider little but your academic firepower. The same is true in Canada and Australia. If you are a talented athlete, it is likely that the US is the land for you.

One last piece of advice for athletes targeting the Ivies. Think about what is motivating the coaches and the competition they face in season and out. Their problem is their competition isn't on or in the field or track or court or pool, it is miles away in their fellow Ivy League coaches' offices. All coaches play the same strategic game and many are targeting the same pool of athletes.

The stakes are high in this contest as coaches risk their reputations on an Ivy League title, or in the case of the less athletic Ivies, not ending up at the bottom of the conference eight. My advice is, if you are being courted by an Ivy or two or three or four or more, remember that the coach who is showing major interest in you is probably also courting, with similar levels of enthusiasm, a lot more athletes than they actually need on their team.

Coaches at schools like Harvard, Princeton, and Yale know that most of their athletes are being wooed by Harvard, Princeton, or Yale, and although coaches may play a pretty honest game, they also hedge their bets trying to hold on to the cream of the crop by encouraging prospective recruits to let them know if they have interest from another Ivy before they make the decision to commit. This gives them an advantage in two ways. First it gives them a sneak peek into the competition's recruitment list and strategy, and second it keeps them on the front foot providing them with the opportunity to make an athlete a verbal offer before the competition swoops in.

Let's face it, if a coach from Harvard says they want you to let them know if another Ivy is making you an offer, chances are you are going to give Harvard a heads up. But that doesn't necessarily guarantee you a place at Harvard. So my advice is, while you're playing with your head, remember the coaches are too. Use your academics and your understanding about the psychology of competition to keep yourself ahead of the game.

Chapter 14

Managing Your Toughest Adversary—Your Mind!

One of the most critical elements to master in the journey of preparing for top universities is your mind.

My competitive streak in academics began in Year 1. I was five years old and thought that school was a pretty fun activity and that given I didn't really have much choice in the matter of whether I went or not, I may as well enjoy it. At the end of the school year, one of my friends received the general excellence prize and I received a prize for "written language." I was quite sure that I could be a strong academic student and could have won this vaguely determined "general excellence prize" and so as Year 2 began, I took my academics extra seriously.

From then on throughout primary school, intermediate school, and high school, my academic goals continued to grow and grow. I remember taking my first set of competitive exams in Year 3 when I was eight years old. Our school began to introduce different streams of mathematics and eventually English and I relished the challenge of being in the more advanced classes.

As I grew up a little, the scoreboard for academic success became increasingly well defined. From about Year 5 onwards, subject prizes were awarded for each academic subject as well as a general excellence prize for the top overall student. I would study fiercely (or as fiercely as one does at the age of 10) for these exams. I fondly remember sitting in Wendy's in Otahuhu with my mother, Paula, and having her test me on the latest history or social studies facts. My aspirations continued to grow when I learned of an award called Dux. This was awarded to the top overall academic student in Year 8. That at the time was my own Everest of academic achievements. I would be inspired by the talented students each year who strode across the stage at prize giving and collected the Dux prize. There were many athletic awards, leadership positions, and more, but for me, the most glorious achievement was being Dux.

I put increasingly higher amounts of pressure on myself each year to perform. I remember in Year 6, I had received an injection of some kind the afternoon before my exam and was having a bit of an adverse reaction to the vaccine. It was impossible to fall asleep and my arm was in quite a bit of pain. The next day, I embarked on a science exam with very little sleep. I ended up scoring 2nd that year overall in my school. To me, it felt like my world had imploded.

Admittedly, the kind of intensity with which I chased my academic goals was definitely unusual. My mother was very good at supporting these ambitions I had, and even championing them. We both figured that the most competitive athletes in the school took great pride in their victories, and would shed tears in their defeats, so academics was my athletics. Every time I went to the exam room, I did it with a kind of competitive zeal and energy. I used my tutors, particularly in mathematics and english, as my own kind of secret weapon. The same way a top tennis player might have a tennis coach, I took great pride in sourcing the best possible tutors at every stage.

I finished Saint Kentigern Prep as Dux and the success fueled my competitive focus even more. As I landed an academic scholarship to a competitive local private high school, King's College, I was determined to build on my academic momentum.

When I first started at King's, my aspiration was to study medicine locally in New Zealand. That was, after all, the peak achievement in academics a young New Zealander could have. I didn't really know what being a doctor would entail, but it seemed to be challenging and I had a knack for science.

As you read earlier in my foreword, this all changed on that day when I sat on a train next to the Dux of King's College, Ben Kornfeld. Ben was a US citizen and as I explained, had recently been admitted to Yale. He told me as a wide-eyed Year 9 student sitting next to him on that train from Glen Innes to Otahuhu that I should consider applying to the United States, as opposed to staying local. This was my Eureka moment. I didn't have any real connection to medicine and I yearned to compete on the world stage. By going to a global university, I could meet ambitious classmates from around the world. It sounded perfect and all I had to do was get in!

As I studied up on the US college process, one thing became clear to me. My academic performance was going to be critical. The United States, unlike applications to Australia or the United Kingdom or New Zealand, puts reasonable focus on your "class rank" or how you are positioned against other students. They also put a lot of focus on to what extent you go above and beyond the standard requirements of your school's academic program. For years, I had worked hard to be the highest ranked academic student at my school, but now with the aspirations to go to a top university like Harvard, I had a reason behind my frenetic focus.

The way my high school worked was almost designed to ignite my competitive streak. All students were streamed into an academic class ranked by their ability. The top class was "R," which historically was called "Removed" because they did different academic material to other students. Classes then went from A1 all the way down to A5. After every term, students were given a term order score across all of their subjects as well as an exam order score (after every exam sitting). This meant that every term, I would know exactly where I stood.

I loved this black-and-white system, but did it make for a particularly relaxing mental state? Absolutely not! I began to view every single test, every week, as a step toward my US college aspirations. Being the strongest academic student wasn't just about pride but became the best bet I had to unlock the global career to which I aspired.

I put myself under intense pressure. Fortunately, I had a lot of positive reinforcement. I finished the first year at my new high school ranked first in my year and winning basically all of the subject prizes. My academic ability had converted well into this new environment.

Fast-forward to Year 13 (my last or senior year in high school), I was putting myself under extreme levels of pressure. I had been first academically for four consecutive years, and I wasn't going to give up one inch on my race to apply to these top universities with the best possible profile. I had amassed a personal army of tutors—in biology, chemistry, physics, mathematics, English, French, and the SAT and various other advisors. I used these tutors to get through hundreds of hours of course content in a much more efficient manner.

I had a particularly talented competitor who was aiming to study in Australia. The criteria for admission to Australian medical schools required only a standardized test called the UMAT (now the UCAT) and four A Levels. I was pursuing 10 A Levels; had launched a variety of clubs; was competing in debating, Model UN, and various athletic areas; was taking a university mathematics course; and had a laundry list of other extracurriculars and obligations.

At the same time, my most critical pillar of my emotional support for all of these years—my family—was being really shaken up by a horrible disease: Alzheimer's. My grandmother Sarah had been struggling with the disease for many years and what had started as some forgetfulness had morphed into not being able to recognize any of us or able to speak. Her medical challenges were heartbreaking for my grandfather John. For much of my early life, he had been my sole male role model and his own mental health started to spiral—the resulting toll coming crashing down on my mother and me. Without going into unnecessary details, I found myself unable to simply blissfully focus on nailing my academics, but I had to really step up and balance a new kind of pressure and obligation during this pressing time. (I have to add here that my grandfather John is now 92 and doing better than ever. He remains a true inspiration to me.)

My final year in high school was easily the most challenging year of my life. It was more challenging than Harvard, Stanford, Oxford, or Yale. It was more challenging than balancing my Harvard degree with an effective full-time role investing at Tiger, a leading hedge fund, and then another effectively full-time role building Crimson. To this day, I literally have the occasional nightmare about my last year in high school.

To handle this pressure in my senior year, I basically stopped hanging out with my friends, eliminated a host of extracurriculars, and tried to minimize my attendance at almost anything that would take time away from my academics and my family.

It strained a lot of my close friendships as many of my classmates, aiming for universities in New Zealand and Australia, had already gained admission into their target degrees and institutions and were celebrating being in their final year of high school knowing what their next step would be. I would turn down social event after social event. Activities like going to a weekend Model United Nations conference and talking to my tutors were some of my only reprieves. It was puritanical but necessary. If I hadn't thrown the kitchen sink at my academic journey, I would have always regretted it.

Having lived through this painful but rewarding journey and then experiencing the absolute euphoria of getting into Harvard in December of 2012, I try to prepare my Crimson students as rigorously as possible for the mental onslaught that high school can bring so they can savor the joys of the process with as little pain as possible. My obligatory all capitals Facebook post on December 13th, 2012, is a good metaphor for the massive release of excitement this moment brought after almost five years (probably longer if you think of the years of academic training beforehand) that led up to the moment (see Figure 14.1).

Over the years observing thousands of the world's most ambitious high school students at Crimson across many different cultural backgrounds, parenting styles, and schooling environments, I have observed various techniques that tend to drive high performance.

First, it is critical that you have some family around you that you can rely on to be an emotional pillar of support during the highs and lows. You will have bad test scores, you will have good test scores. You will feel like you got

Figure 14.1

Source: Jamie Beaton (Author)

punched in the guts when you didn't get the leadership role you hoped for and euphoric when a surprise accolade comes your way. You will have breakthroughs in your extracurriculars after periods in which it seemed like your momentum was slowing. You will encounter difficult academic concepts that make you doubt you have the ability to keep going. Your family support system will cheer you on through thick and thin and act as an anchor for your mental health.

Second, you aren't going to get into these colleges by relaxing, and you need to be at peace with this. You can't win the Olympics without blood, sweat, and tears. The students who get in when the acceptance rate at a place like Harvard is under 4%[1] are by definition the exception not the norm. You are going to put a lot of strain on your internal systems to go after this goal and you need to. This is the same experience that thousands of ambitious students across the US and the globe are living.

Third, you need to put yourself in a position of optimal pressure. If you feel school is too easy, you should be taking more subjects, going faster, taking more extracurriculars, or setting more ambitious goals. If you feel so overwhelmed that you see your grades falling, you can't keep up with your commitments, and your family is telling you that you don't seem yourself, you are putting yourself under too much pressure. The trick (and this is an art not a science) is to continually push yourself but not so much that you will snap. You ultimately will be the best barometer for how you are progressing, but use your family and friends as an indicator for this as well.

Fourth, eliminate all the activities you can that you don't enjoy. People often ask me about my time management strategies. Time is important, but what I find really burns through people's stamina are activities they don't enjoy.

As I mentioned, I used to hate guitar so much that I would hide from my guitar teacher during my morning tea lessons. Although I initially enjoyed karate, I began to dread the sessions. The psychological pain of doing an activity or an academic subject you really don't enjoy goes far beyond the time commitment. It will affect your mood, your energy levels, and your happiness. You can't drop everything. For example, everyone needs to achieve a reasonable level of success in mathematics to do well in things like the SAT. Many activities, however, are at your full discretion and you can drop what you don't enjoy.

Fifth, find a niche you can thrive in and dominate it. We are wired to feed off positive feedback, peer recognition, and success. If you are indifferent between accounting and US history but you can be the best student in your school in accounting because there is less competition, take accounting. The thrill of picking up prizes in the field, being recognized by your teachers, and mastering the content will give you the self-confidence and energy you need to handle your challenges in other areas.

Sixth, celebrate all your successes. Every time you get a good test score or achieve a new milestone on your marathon preparation in your college admissions journey, tell your best friend about it, tell your parents about it, tell your siblings about it, and take a moment to appreciate it. Your successes fuel positive momentum that can feed your commitment to studying, academic discipline and give you more desire to push harder and increase your potential pressure capacity.

Seventh, get enough sleep. One of my recent admits to Harvard took 17 AP subjects, got two patents, won multiple Olympiads, launched multiple clubs, played various sports, achieved multiple music diplomas and a laundry list of other achievements. He got good sleep every night and maintained a healthy diet. If you aren't getting enough sleep, seek some expert advice on how you can re-optimize your schedule, adjust your academic program, or choose new extracurriculars. It is critical that you get six to eight hours of sleep a day. I won't pretend you will always get eight hours. I didn't and you won't. You can, however, generally commit to sleeping properly as many nights as you can. This is important for your mental health, physical health, and also your cognition levels. If you are too sleepy, you will struggle to remember content, engage in class, or connect with your friends socially. You will be cranky and get angry over small, irrelevant things. Prioritize sleep.

Eight, play sports every week. Of the more than 370+ students I have sent to the Ivy League, I can't recall one who played no sports. You may be a terrible athlete. I was marginal at best (although I certainly tried my best), but you still need to participate. Physical activity is great for your mental health and stress release. You will generally sleep better and perform at a higher standard if you incorporate some sports into your schedule.

Ninth, eat well. I won't pretend that I always stuck to this. My diet in high school was pretty atrocious. At one point, I used to get Burger King for breakfast multiple times a week. Luckily my metabolism was strong. As I've gotten a little older, I have changed my diet (in a good way) quite dramatically and I've found I have much higher energy levels, better focus, and I basically feel a lot happier. If you pour rocket fuel into your system, it will lead to rocket fuel–inspired academic results! Bad eating erodes some of the benefits of good sleep and physical exercise. For peak performance, exercise well; sleep at normal, consistent levels; and eat well!

Finally, don't place unnecessary stress on yourself. There are some moments when it is game on. When I sat my final exams and knew that the winner of Dux (valedictorian) of my high school would rest on who performed better in various two-hour assessments, there was no way to escape the stress that comes with that kind of focus. I had to perform and the pressure I felt was in line with what I wanted to achieve. For things such as the SAT, you can meaningfully reduce your stress because you can re-sit it several times. It doesn't need to feel like life or death because if you have a bad test result or perform poorly in a certain section, you can just give it another go.

Similarly, start as early as possible. If I did it again, I would start the journey from the age of 10 or 11. Many of my students begin taking Advanced Placement exams when they are 13 or 14 (at our online high school we enroll students based on ability, not age). This is great because it spaces out exams over more years, gives you more opportunities for re-sits, and avoids enormous pressure and multiple high-stakes activities in the same months of your final year.

Usually the strongest students reduce as much of the pressure as possible through early preparation, spacing out key exams, and carefully managing their commitments and schedule.

As a top student, you need to weaponize your toughest adversary, your mind! Being self-aware, establishing powerful support systems around you, early planning, and knowing your own capacity for pressure is integral in charting a successful path through the college admissions arena of high school.

Chapter 15

International Students and the Even More Uneven Playing Field

In an ideal world, the most brilliant higher education institutions such as Harvard, Stanford, and Yale would be represented by students whose demographics mirror the world. US residents represent a little over 4% of the world[1] so one could imagine 4% of incoming students would come from the US. This, of course, varies enormously from reality and is unlikely to ever happen. These great institutions are, after all, US institutions. They receive substantial federal support and primarily serve US students. At Harvard University, approximately 85% of incoming freshmen are US students.[2]

One of the reasons these institutions have become such bastions of academic excellence in recent years, however, is that the students who aspire to gain a coveted seat don't just reside in the US. There has been a steady growth in applicants from all corners of the world, with particularly large representation from regions such as China, India, and Korea.[3] The obsession with the US colleges is not unreasonable. In the *U.S. News* Global University Rankings, eight of the world's top ten universities are in the United States.[4]

Many students ask me if the location you apply from affects your odds of admission. It absolutely does. It has a major effect. In fact, it is substantially harder to get into the best universities in the US if you apply as an international student. If you thought it was hard to get into one of these top schools as an US resident, you wouldn't believe how the competition steps up once you foray into the international student landscape.

Crimson has been a fascinating lens to watch this trend evolve with our offices across more than 20 countries. From Russia to Japan to Korea to Brazil to Australia to New Zealand to India to China to the UK and South Africa, we have a unique vantage point into the global preparation journey of students aspiring to leave their home country and boldly venture to the US for their higher education.

On average, our analysis at Crimson shows it is two to three times harder for international students to gain admission into a university than a domestic peer.

MIT disclosed in the class of 2024 an acceptance rate for international students of 3.4% compared to 8.2% for domestic applications.[5] This trend has continued for several years. In the Class of 2023, the acceptance rate for international students was 3.1% compared to a domestic acceptance rate of 7.6%.[6] Even for the class of 2020, the acceptance rate for international students was only 3.1% compared to 9.4% for domestic applicants.[7]

The trend continues across the Ivy League. The University of Pennsylvania released that their international acceptance rate for the Class of 2024 was 6.1% for international students compared to 9.6% for US students.[8] For the class of 2022, this was 5.9% for international students and 8.2% for US students.[9] For the class of 2019, this was 6.6% for international students and 10.2% overall for US students.[10]

Moving along to New Jersey, Princeton released data for the class of 2022 showing international students had an acceptance rate of 3.6% compared to 5.9% for domestic applicants.[11] This trend has actually stayed consistent for more than 20 years. For the Class of 2010, the acceptance rate was 6.3% for international students but 10.9% for US students.[12] For the Class of 2005, the acceptance rate was 5.6% for international students but 12.9% for US students.[13] In the 1996 class, the acceptance rate was 4.5% for international students but 13.0% for US students.[14]

The Ivy Leagues may have a preference for domestic applicants but what about the most famous public university system in the US?

A similar trend is seen at UC Berkeley. It disclosed that for the class of 2023, international acceptance rates were 9.14% compared to 17.1% for domestic students.[15] For the class of 2022, international acceptance rates were 8.7% compared to 16.6% for domestic students.[16] For the class of 2021, international acceptance rates were 8.6% compared to 20.4% for US students.[17]

UC Berkeley also fortunately releases data showing that international students outrank domestic students on all of the quantifiable metrics (mostly grades and test scores). For international students in the Class of 2023, the 25th to 75th percentile SAT range was 1450–1530.[18] Because the

25th to 75th percentile range is 1330–1530 for the whole student body (for the Class of 2024 but the statistics are comparable),[19] the 25th percentile international student is roughly as good as the 50th percentile student overall. You see a similar story with the ACT, where the international student range is 32–35[20] and the overall range is 29–35.[21]

What does this mean for you? Rejoice if you are a US domestic applicant and wince if you are an international student!

In all seriousness, you do face stiffer competition as an international student. It is worth noting that these numbers may appear difficult, but the reality is likely even more challenging. The awareness of the US application process is naturally much greater within the US than globally. As a result, most qualified applicants are likely to apply within the US. Internationally, there may still be many talented students who never consider applying to US universities. Only a highly motivated, well-informed segment of students is actually likely to end up applying to the US as opposed to staying and attending local university options.

If you grow up in a country like Australia, there are plenty of reasonable domestic university options such as the University of Sydney, the University of New South Wales, the University of Melbourne, or the Australian National University in the country's capital of Canberra. As a result, the pool of students who end up actually applying is likely to be highly self-selecting. This should imply, if all else was held constant, that an international applicant on average may be stronger than a domestic applicant and as a result, should be admitted at a higher rate. In reality, across almost all the schools I analyzed, the international acceptance rate is much lower. As a result, you are really facing an uphill battle on many fronts as an international student.

That said, as an international student, there is much you can do to boost your odds. Beyond many of the tactics I have described so far, you should make sure, where possible, to take an international curriculum that is well recognized such as A Levels or Advanced Placement. You should almost certainly take the SAT even if it is an optional test. Our data suggests that those with SAT scores—even in a test optional universe—continue to be admitted at a substantially higher rate. Additionally, it is all the more important that you strive to be the best possible student within your high school environment. Many of our 25 global admits to Harvard and Stanford in 2021 were ranked in the top three of their high school class.

Another tip is, when possible, you should compete in global competitions that directly benchmark you against US students. One of my recent Harvard admits from China was an international finalist in the INTEL Science and Engineering Fair. This type of competition provides a US admissions officer with an easy benchmark to evaluate his ability against domestic applicants. This is important because the more unfamiliar your qualifications and extracurriculars are, the more the achievements are likely to be discounted. By competing in well-recognized qualifications and tournaments, you will make the admissions officer's job easier for them by demystifying your candidacy and academic ability so they can more easily advocate for you.

An additional factor to think about is the differential impact of financial aid on international students. Traditionally, most US universities have substantially more financial aid available for domestic applicants than international students. This is true, even at Ivy League schools like Columbia, The University of Pennsylvania, and Cornell. These great institutions continue to be need-aware which means that if you apply for financial aid, it makes it harder to get in as an international applicant. As a result, make sure you really need financial aid before ticking the box to apply for. It immediately drops your potential to be accepted quite meaningfully across all but the most well-resourced US universities.

Although the stats may appear ugly, we have sent thousands of talented international students to leading US universities over the last eight years. It is definitely achievable but you need to know transparently the race you are running. You need to start early and you need to be prepared.

As an international student myself, I continue to hope that in the Harvard admissions cycle of 2042, you will see an international student admit rate that more closely proxies the domestic US admit rate. I can't help but think that equity in admission to these institutions, which can catapult people up social classes and accelerate their global careers, ideally goes beyond the borders of the US.

At a certain point, when institutions like Harvard and Stanford possess such power to unlock careers of distinction in their incoming classmates, do they become a public good of sorts? Should the benefits accrue primarily to US citizens or to citizens of the world?

It is not my place to answer these philosophical questions. Today, I am here to help you get in. It is, however, most certainly a debate worth having.

Chapter 16

Moneyball
How to Rank and Choose the Best Universities

So far, I have focused on equipping you with tips, tricks, and insights to boost your odds at gaining admission into the world's best universities. In this chapter, I will help you figure out which are actually the world's best universities so when you have the choices on the table, you can make the best decision!

You would think that after all these years the major ranking organizations have figured this out. On the whole, they do a pretty good job, and I have great respect for the caliber and reputation of major organizations like *U.S. News* and *Times Higher Education*. One thing I have noticed, however, is that many of these university ranking organizations have their roots in postgraduate rankings. As a result, peculiar trends arise in their undergraduate rankings that really don't reflect reality.

A funny example of this: Princeton. I like Princeton and enjoyed the preview days after high school when I was assessing colleges. Princeton has been ranked number one by *U.S. News* for more than 10 consecutive years.[1] There are various reasons for this. They have a large endowment per student. They have very high rates of alumni giving. They perform well on all the classic measurements of academic success like average SAT scores and more.

The funny thing is though, I have never met a student who has chosen Princeton over Harvard, Stanford, or MIT. The idea that Princeton would sit on top of these universities for so many years is just one such example of the slightly bizarre disconnect between what students actually choose when they have the choice and what the rankings say.

In this chapter, I'll equip you with some simple mathematics and economic analysis to be able to assess what are actually the best universities in the world and a general decision-making framework to help you choose what college you want to go to.

First, we start with yield. The yield is the percentage of students admitted by a university that ultimately ends up getting accepted by a university. I introduced this concept to you previously and it is an important one. We all want to get into these top universities. Yield measures if we actually end up going when faced with a choice. The best universities such as Harvard and Stanford have yield rates higher than 80% (2020). Cornell, an Ivy League school, has a yield rate of 60% (2020).[2] The higher the yield rate, the better the university (in other words, the yield rate is positively correlated with the quality of the university).

Next up, the acceptance rate. As the name suggests, this is the percentage of students who are admitted to a university from those who apply. Generally, the inverse of the acceptance rate is a proxy for the quality of the university.

The lower the acceptance rate, the better the university (in other words, the acceptance rate is negatively correlated with the quality of the university). (See Figure 16.1.)

The final definition we need is the cross-yield. The cross-yield measures the percentage of students who choose one school over another one when they are faced with the choice. For example, Harvard is estimated to have cross-yield of 54% with Stanford. This means that 54% of students admitted to both Harvard and Stanford choose Harvard.[3] This is very important because, ultimately, you are going to need to compare two schools.

Traditionally, rankings use measurements like number of publications, faculty size, selectivity of the school, and other factors in a multivariable regression to order schools. The problem is most of these variables really have very little to do with what drives a student to ultimately choose a school. They do provide a proxy for the quality of the university, but in my opinion it is not the cleanest measure.

As to why, we now take a quick detour to the world of Wall Street. In finance, the stock market is the holy grail

Figure 16.1

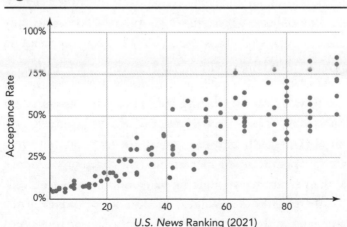

of market efficiency. A theory called the "efficient market hypothesis" won Eugene Fama the Nobel Prize for arguing that it is impossible to "beat the market." What this means is that an individual stock investor (you or I) should not generally be able to go out and study various stocks, choose a set of them, and have them beat the market on average.

There is a lot of complexity to this we won't dwell on today, but the nuts and bolts is that the crowd has a lot of wisdom. All the people buying and selling in the stock market have information about the different prospects of a company. As a result, the aggregate price that comes from all of this buying and selling is likely to be very precise. The price may of course move in the future; for example, a company may have a surprise discovery of a new oil mine or a new breakthrough electric vehicle and the stock price may shoot up, but it is nearly impossible to systematically beat the market.

Every time someone consults a *U.S. News* Ranking or a *QS World University Ranking*, they are essentially performing the role of an individual stock picker, studying various data. A company may have profits, revenue, competitors, and a corporate strategy. A university has its faculty, publication rates, endowment size, and various other factors. Using a ranking consisting of so many factors is actually overcomplicating things significantly and actually resulting in worse outcomes.

The best way to rank universities is to use the wisdom of the crowds. Instead of using individual rankings based on certain characteristics, it is better to use the collective hive mind of tens of thousands of smart students who every year are forced to choose between different colleges. They have a lot at stake. They are going to spend four years of their life there. They are going to spend a lot of money. They are going to use their degree to enter the job market. As a result, their collective decision-making is likely to encompass more information and value for a prospective college student than a static ranking.

Any factor such as the rate at which faculty publish only becomes relevant to a prospective college student to the extent it will actually affect their experience. If it does, then this information will ultimately filter into information like the yield rate and the cross-yield rate. If it is irrelevant to the prospective college student, then it will create a point of error in the ranking whereby a student may actually have a different preference.

Using a ranking based on the wisdom of the crowd is akin to the efficient market hypothesis for the stock market. It is better to rest on the collective wisdom of thousands than trying to redo the analysis for yourself. By all means, don't just choose a college based on a ranking. However, it is totally valid to start with a wisdom of the crowd ranking as the most accurate representation of what the typical student would do and then personalize your decision-making from there.

As such, I provide you with two powerful rankings that actually capture the best universities more effectively than current rankings that don't use the wisdom of the crowds in its purest sense.

This first ranking looks at the top US universities and evaluates them in pairs (see Table 16.1). If you were presented with two colleges to choose from, what would you choose? Harvard versus Princeton? Stanford versus Columbia? MIT versus Caltech? I move through the list of universities and consider these pairwise relationships. If Harvard tends to win more students than Stanford in a head-to-head comparison, then Harvard is ranked higher.

This ranking reveals a list that much more closely resembles what I see on the ground from thousands of students

Table 16.1 Ranking 1: Cross-Yield Ranking

Name	Based on Cross-Yield Data (2018)	Based on *U.S. News* (2021)
Harvard	1	2
Stanford	2	6
MIT	3	4
Yale	4	4
Princeton	5	1
Caltech	6	9
Columbia	7	3
UPenn	8	8
Duke	9	12
UChicago	10	6
Brown	11	14
Dartmouth	12	13
Northwestern	13	9
Cornell	14	18
Georgetown	15	23
Rice	16	16
Johns Hopkins	17	9
Notre Dame	18	19
WashU	19	16
Vanderbilt	20	14

choosing their university options each year. Stanford is ranked sixth in the *U.S. News* 2021 ranking[4] but for a significant portion of California is the dream university. Many of my clients in California who work in leadership positions at major technology companies don't mention Harvard as they talk about their aspirations for their children—Stanford is the name. I have seen a growing number of applicants in China and Korea who aspire to work in the STEM field placing Stanford at the top of their list. The idea that Stanford is the sixth best college in the US makes very little sense. I haven't yet met a student who chose to go to Yale or Princeton over Stanford for their undergraduate degree.

As an applicant, you want to be concerned about the reputation and the ranking of your university in the eyes of fellow students and employers. This is going to be a big driver of the set of career opportunities you can access on graduation. You are often told by your career counselors and other people to not worry about rankings. In my experience, this is more of a counseling technique used to alleviate stress and pressure than actually useful advice.

If you are a student who aspires to go into venture capital and you end up at Stanford compared to UCLA, it will meaningfully affect your first job prospects. I would say it is luxurious to pretend rankings don't matter. Functionally, every student I meet consults rankings as their first and foremost criteria and I think there is nothing wrong with that. You are going to bear the mark of your school for your career and will be directly and indirectly affected by its reputation.

Using this ranking framework, Princeton drops down to the fifth position. This makes a lot of sense because generally people prefer Harvard, Stanford, MIT, and Yale over Princeton. As such, it would be unusual for a candidate to choose Princeton over the other schools. The *U.S. News* ranking might give you the impression people do, but in reality, they rarely do.

Another interesting example is Duke. In the *U.S. News* ranking, Northwestern is ranked quite a bit higher than Duke (9th compared to 12th). I have similarly never heard of any of my students choosing Northwestern over Duke.

Generally when it comes to universities, a lot of the reputational value of a university is indirectly based on the perception of everybody else of that university. As a result, you can choose to ignore cross-yield data if you really want to, but you need to be very confident as to your decision-making. I usually advise my students to trust the wisdom of the crowds.

To construct the cross-yield ranking, an economics principle called "transitivity" becomes relevant. What is transitivity? Imagine someone asks you if you like McDonalds, Burger King, or KFC more and you say the following: I like McDonalds more than Burger King. I like Burger King more than KFC. I like KFC more than McDonalds. Take a second to read this. Do you see the problem?

1. McDonalds > Burger King
2. Burger King > KFC
3. KFC > McDonalds

If (1) and (2) is true, then McDonalds > KFC because McDonalds > Burger King > KFC. However, (3) gives us the opposite, that is, KFC > McDonalds. You have a logical paradox, an impossible relationship. Transitivity is an assumption that preferences are consistent across all pairs, such that if A > B and B > C then A > C.

You can tell that the cross-yield rankings are quite powerful because the laws of transitivity almost perfectly hold across the top-10 universities. It is hard to find many scenarios with multiple choices (in this case 10) where transitivity holds. The fact that the consistency of preferences between the universities holds means you can put extra credibility in the ranking. The only exception in the top-10 where transitivity breaks down is Caltech-UChicago. UChicago wins in cross-yield at 56% against Caltech but Caltech is ranked a bit higher because of its performance against other universities. Interestingly, UPenn has a high cross-yield against MIT (46% appear to choose UPenn over

MIT) and it is a dead race between UPenn and Caltech (50%–50%).

The efficacy of cross-yield as a ranking tool falls as you look at lower ranked universities. This is because if you ask someone if they prefer Harvard over Brown, the choice is generally pretty consistent. However, as you compare say Pepperdine and UC Davis, it is very uncertain what is actually better and your individual major preferences, desires for location, housing, professors, and other considerations may tilt people either way. As a result, transitivity tends to break down more and more as you head down the list of universities and the "wisdom of the crowd" loses some of its clarity in what is the best option.

I'll give you a final tool to analyze universities. This is a special Crimson concoction that also works very well. Here I rank universities based on the yield rate/acceptance rate. I call this "yield-adjusted acceptance rate."

This is powerful because the acceptance rate alone is very powerful but can be gamed. For example, there is an online university called the Minerva Project. This is a start-up university that has for many years made claims to have acceptance rates below 5%. To this day, I have never met a student who has ever chosen the Minerva Project over a major reputable US university. I've also never met a student who has been rejected by the Minerva Project. I am skeptical of their acceptance data, but even if it is accurate and they just seem to love every student I've ever seen applying, it is important to know if students end up accepting offers.

Walmart is another funny example. A viral news article stated that Walmart had an acceptance rate of 2% and was more selective than Harvard. Most people would generally prefer to be at Harvard than working at Walmart. Factors like the yield rate help to capture who actually turns up and accepts their offer.

Yield is positively correlated with good universities and is determined by the student choice to accept an offer. Acceptance rate is negatively correlated with good universities and is determined by the university's choice to make an offer. This weighting of yield-adjusted acceptance rate is subsequently quite hard to game because it captures market feedback from both universities and students (note that UChicago appears to have been able to do this, but they seem to be the only exception). Table 16.2 is my second ranking for you.

This ranking is useful because yield rate and acceptance rate data is published quite readily so you can easily run this ranking yourself in Excel no matter whether you read this in 2024, 2042, or hot off the press in 2022. If you have the data, I prefer cross-yield because it captures the real choices that students make between different universities, which is more useful for a comparative analysis like a ranking.

This ranking is generally very solid. It ranks the Ivy League well. (1) Harvard, (2) Princeton, (3) Columbia, (4) Yale, (5) UPenn, (6) Brown, (7) Dartmouth, (8) Cornell broadly tracks the general preferences I see in most students. The ranking of Columbia is contentious. Some students love it because of its location in New York City, which is a huge perk. Generally, most people would regard Yale as being a better choice than Columbia, but the location of Yale in New Haven is a bit of a drawback compared to the thriving urban metropolis of the city that never sleeps.

One issue with ranking universities based on acceptance rate is that it tends to penalize MIT and Caltech. Both of these universities are specialized engineering schools. As a result, a far smaller cross section of students can apply in the first place than to a school like Harvard, which has majors from economics to engineering to folklore and mythology (yes, I have a student preparing to apply for it this major).

Table 16.2 Ranking 2: Yield-Adjusted Acceptance Rate

Name	Based on Yield-Adjusted Acceptance Rate (2020)	Based on *U.S. News* (2021)
Stanford	1	6
Harvard	2	2
UChicago	3	6
Princeton	4	1
MIT	5	4
Columbia	6	3
Yale	7	4
UPenn	8	8
Brown	9	14
Dartmouth	10	13
Duke	11	12
Caltech	12	9
Northwestern	13	9
Cornell	14	18
Vanderbilt	15	14
Rice	16	16
Johns Hopkins	17	9
USC	18	24
Notre Dame	19	19
UCLA	20	20

As a result, a methodology that considers only acceptance rate will underestimate the caliber of MIT because it has a smaller pool to draw on in the first place. This is partially addressed in our ranking by addressing the yield rate because a university like MIT should have a very high yield rate among the admitted pool of engineering students. MIT has a yield rate of 77%, which is very close to Harvard and Stanford and higher than any other Ivy League school. Caltech gets penalized when it comes to yield because a lot of the students who get admitted to Caltech also get into MIT and generally will choose MIT. As a result, Caltech needs a bit more love in the rankings than a purely yield-based metric will generally apply.

I have used these ranking frameworks to extensive lengths in my own decision-making, most recently when I chose between Harvard and Yale Law School. In 2021, Harvard Law School had a yield rate of 54%. Harvard Law School had an acceptance rate of 12.49%. Yale Law School had a yield rate of 70% and an acceptance rate of 8.22%. Applying our formulas, this gives Harvard a score of $0.54/0.1249 = 4.32$. It gives Yale a score of $0.70/0.0822 = 8.51$. Although I was entranced by Harvard Law School for many reasons, I looked at the statistics and confidently chose Yale. Although I may miss Elle Woods, I haven't looked back.

Who are the biggest winners and losers of our refined ranking methodologies?

1. Princeton, Columbia, UChicago, and Northwestern drop four places from their *U.S. News* rankings when using cross-yield.

2. Stanford rises four places, and Caltech, Duke, and Brown rise three places when using their cross-yield ranking.

3. Johns Hopkins drops eight places from its *U.S. News* ranking when using cross-yield or yield-adjusted acceptance rates.

4. Georgetown rises eight places when using cross-yield rankings.

5. Emory drops five places from its *U.S. News* ranking when using cross-yield rates and 10 places using yield-adjusted acceptance rates.

6. Washington University in St Louis appears to have a bit of magic. Perhaps Carrie Bradshaw would agree if you've seen her blockbusters lately. They do surprisingly well in both cross-yield and yield-adjusted acceptance rates at about 50% against strong schools like Stanford and Brown. This is likely because of location preferences and their strong scholarship programs.

7. UChicago, who through their creative use of two types of admissions (one binding, one nonbinding) across early and regular admission and their fantastically complicated essays have been the master engineers of hacking *U.S. News*. Our yield-adjusted acceptance rates capture their great economic engineering of the admissions process: they rise three places to third when assessed through this lens. Stanford rises five places to first when considering yield-adjusted acceptance rates.

8. NYU and USC rise six places when using yield-adjusted acceptance rates. Tufts rises seven places.

The benefit of using a wisdom-of-the-crowds approach to help you choose what university to attend is you will never go far wrong. Your decisions are building on the collective wisdom of thousands of sophisticated university applicants and their parents which are captured by cross-yield and yield-adjusted acceptance rate. Use these powerful mathematical tools to make the best college decision possible!

Chapter 17

Harvard's Legacy, My Legacy, and Your Legacy

One of the most peculiar aspects of the US college system is legacy. As a young boy in New Zealand, I was often told by people and was quite sad to hear that "life is about who you know rather than what you know." As a student who was learning a lot but didn't really know anyone, this was fairly depressing wisdom. I wasn't necessarily the most social, I didn't have the most friends, but I did have hard work on my side. A system where pure merit and being able to just pour in the effort yielded the best results suited me just fine. The US college system isn't quite as clean cut.

I didn't fully appreciate what legacy admissions meant when I was applying, and I figured I had many cards stacked against me anyway, what did one more card matter?

If you sit back, pull up a cup of tea, and really reflect for a moment, legacy admissions sound somewhat ridiculous. Legacy admissions refers to the system in which colleges grant the children of alumni special privileges in the admissions process. Essentially, if your dad went there, you have a much higher shot of getting in. According to *The Guardian newspaper*, in 2019 Harvard legacy students had an admission rate of 33%.[1] This gives some of the US colleges a vibe that is more like some kind of exclusive business society or golf club than a holy grail of meritocracy drawing the talented students from far corners of society into the careers they are most equipped for.

Before you jump off your chair and knock over your tea, consider a few things. First, parents who studied at Harvard are likely to be higher income, with more education and perhaps have more motivation than the average person whose child is applying to college. They are more likely to have fostered an academic culture at home that encouraged their children to perform. They may have higher natural IQ levels and may have passed this on to their children. They may be more familiar with the application process and be in a stronger position to help their children navigate it.

As a result, you can't assume the pool of general applicants to Harvard and the pool of legacy applicants to Harvard are the same. Although the legacy pool may have had the aforementioned advantages, the average general student will more than likely be academically and extracurricularly superior than their legacy counterparts.

Second, depending on your philosophical lens, you may want to consider the utilitarian benefits of legacy admissions. Legacy admissions incentives families to try and send multiple generations through the same institution. This feeds a sense of tradition, loyalty, and community. This in part helps to contribute to the high levels of alumni donations, a common aspect of the US college system. All of these donations help to fund financial aid programs, more research resources, better faculty, and other types of student-centric programs.

There are many criticisms that all the donations that go to elite universities are a waste of "altruism" and perhaps are more egotistical in nature. Recognizing all these arguments, I was still delighted as a student in my first year at Harvard to receive more than $US40 thousand in financial aid. It made the tuition bill affordable for my family. Without these massive endowments and the complicated incentives that drive the giving that feeds them, I might not have been able to study at Harvard in the first place.

The UK, which has no legacy admissions, has incredibly historic universities like Oxford and Cambridge. These universities have endowments that are generally 20% or less than their US equivalents.[2] The lack of legacy admissions doesn't fully explain this vast difference in endowments, but it is one of the factors that makes the US's most elite institutions fundraising machines like no other country.

In 2021, the state of Colorado announced a ban on consideration of the legacy status of students for admission to their public universities.[3] As general skepticism of systems that tend to drive inherent inequality grows, the pressure will grow on the system of legacy admissions to be eliminated.

My conception of legacy is very different.

My obsession with education started with my grandfather, John Beaton. John grew up in unrelenting, working class poverty in Montrose, Scotland. He was a very talented academic student with grades that meant he would have been able to win a scholarship to the Montrose Academy.

Tragically, there wasn't even enough money in the family to afford the uniform costs. The big focus in the family at the time was to see that the children were educated to age 14, after which they would leave school to find work so that they could help support the household. My granddad John and my grandmother Sarah didn't want to bring up children in Britain's tough class system. They took the plunge and went to New Zealand more than 60 years ago as a way of giving their children new education opportunities neither of them had had. My grandmother helped to pay the bills by working in a local potato chip factory. My grandfather worked as a sailor for the Merchant Navy and then as a welder.

My mother grew up with minimal economic resources but cheered on by my grandparents, she passionately chased after the best schooling she could receive. After close to 30 rejections, she found a school, Epsom Girls Grammar, one of the strongest schools in Auckland, that was willing to read her out-of-zone application. She earned three university degrees in rapid succession across law, management, and accounting while university education was free. She worked every summer since she was 15 years old to help bring in money to keep the family humming.

My mother went through a difficult divorce just as she was bringing me into the world and had to balance a little baby as a single mother while trying to get her business off the ground. She made substantive sacrifices to send me to outstanding institutions. We were a team. I took my studies very seriously and competed for every scholarship I could get in New Zealand's best private schools—Saint Kentigern School and King's College—to make sure I was placing as little strain on her as possible. My mother has a kind of otherworldly work ethic that is so sewn into her character, even as she passes 60 years young, she only seems to speed up! Surrounded by that kind of intensity and inspiration, how could I not follow in her hardworking footsteps?

Growing up my granddad, now 92 and thriving, had only heard of Oxford. Oxford was the institution that the elite society of the UK would go to get their degrees at a time when he wasn't given the opportunity to finish high school. Telling my grandad more than 65 years after he left the United Kingdom to give his children more opportunity that I had won a Rhodes Scholarship to Oxford was a special moment for my family.

After I turned 18 and was admitted to Harvard, my mother no longer had to financially support me. A couple of thousand dollars arrived in my bank account from a University of Auckland Scholarship. I began tutoring students in Auckland in the earliest days of Crimson and felt the empowerment of being able to buy my own Oporto burgers without asking my family for support.

In my second year at Harvard, I no longer qualified for financial aid because of the growth of Crimson and my new job at a hedge fund, Tiger Management. Today, I am in a privileged position because of the growth and success of Crimson all over the world. When I am criticized for our focus on the world's best institutions or for pushing privileged opportunities that are hard to access to students across different countries, I am listening, but I wholeheartedly disagree.

Education is the most powerful way to create your own legacy. Few things in life can lead you to stratospherically jump from social class to social class as quickly as an education from one of the world's best institutions. Many of our students have immigrant families who make substantial sacrifices to support the ambition of their children, just as my mother did for me.

The whole reason we introduced programs like Crimson Access Opportunity and other internal scholarships was so that students like Julian, an informatics talent from one of the poorest areas of Mexico, could gain admission to schools like Stanford. Many families forgo material goods, travel, cars, and may have to ask for support from their extended family to invest in their child's education. But what better gift is there? Gratefully, this is exactly what my family did and what they would do all over again for me.

When I meet a young student who is intensely competitive, ambitious, and just wants to know what they need to do to maximize their odds at getting into the best universities, I couldn't be more excited. This system—with its seemingly dichotomous legacy admits and alumni donations, financial aid, and equal opportunity focus—isn't a system I designed or my students designed, but it is what it is, and helping you crack it will help you realize your wildest ambitions.

I am honestly excited about helping you do just that.

Chapter 18

The Personalities of the Ivy Leagues and Which One May Be Right for You

In New Zealand, we have a cultural phenomenon called the "tall poppy syndrome." Tall poppy syndrome is a social mindset in which people that are perceived to be better than average and ambitious, with a string of achievements to their name, are cut down. "Cutting down the tall poppy" results in an environment where high achievers can feel a sense of a growing negative energy toward them from those who are jealous and/or angry to see those extraordinary individuals pushing against the grain. I hate tall poppy syndrome.

In my home country, Crimson has been fortunate to catalyze a nationwide shift among the most ambitious kids in the country to looking global. No longer do top students only consider domestic universities and accept the advice of their local careers counselors. Students come to us and we are able to champion their wildest ambitions, help them find powerful mentors, and accelerate their academic trajectory.

I think of Soumil Singh, one of my earliest students from a public school called Hamilton Boys High School, which primarily teaches the fairly weak national New Zealand curriculum. Soumil came to us at the beginning of high school. We immediately saw his aptitude for mathematics, capacity for leadership, and strong academic fundamentals. He took AP Computer Science with Crimson, went on to take six additional A-Level subjects and a laundry list of scholarship exams. He went on to achieve Top in the World in A-Level Business Studies and A-Level English Language, two subjects he had been taught entirely outside of his traditional school. He won a premier scholarship ranking him in the top 10 in the nation.

Soumil wasn't just amplifying his academics. He became head of the student government, launched a regional initiative to bring together student leaders from a wide variety of schools, and spearheaded a tutoring program for younger students. He landed on the front page of our national newspaper, the *New Zealand Herald*, after he gained admission to four Ivy League schools, including Harvard and Columbia, and his story inspired waves of students across the country to be bolder.[1] He eventually landed at Harvard—the passion in computer science he discovered while working with Crimson progressing to becoming his major (applied mathematics–computer science).

He went on to work for Bridgewater, the world's largest hedge fund led by Ray Dalio, and then on graduating he took one of the most exciting plunges: entrepreneurship. Last year Soumil applied and was accepted into Y-Combinator, the world's leading start-up accelerator, based in San Francisco, which has spawned many unicorns (private billion-dollar companies) like Brex, Airbnb, and DoorDash. At the age of 23, he had received YC-funding and became the CEO of his own tech start-up.

He went from Hamilton, New Zealand, at the age of 16 to being a Silicon Valley start-up CEO in his early 20s backed by fantastic investors. This is the transformative potential of taking a competitive, strategic, and high-intensity approach to high school followed by studying at a world-leading university.

I hate tall poppy syndrome. So does Soumil and so do our thousands of students who just want to put in the hard work and realize their ambitions. It is important to realize that the students who make it all the way into these top universities didn't just perform well in academics. They often ignored incorrect advice suggesting they take fewer subjects or go easier on extracurriculars. They pushed back against friends who told them to stop "trying so hard." They chose hard work when others chose to relax in their pivotal years in high school.

As a Kiwi, I love the US because of its burning ambition. In my first week at Harvard, I met more students who told me they wanted to be the president of the United States than I'd met in my entire life who wanted to "enter politics" in New Zealand. The US has a rep for being overconfident or even arrogant, and from time to time, that may be true. But I think it's worth it. Leading US universities have an infectious energy spiraling around campus that induces this feeling that no ambition is unrealistic, no goal is too ridiculous, and no problem can't eventually be solved. Students soak up that psyche and sentiment of the people around them.

Countries like New Zealand that don't inspire lofty ambition in their youth indirectly pay a debt on all their best people who are knocked down several notches because of the tall poppy syndrome. A culture of possibility will always beat a culture of impossibility. It is important to know the culture of the university you are heading to as it will indirectly have a meaningful impact on your performance, satisfaction, and results.

As long as the US remains the land of possibility, and its institutions of higher education the ultimate launching pads, it will continue to dominate global university rankings and indicators of entrepreneurship and technology leadership.

Although the US generally has a culture of possibility, what are the specific personalities of the top US schools? How will you feel immersed in these cultures? What are the quirks and idiosyncratic nuances? I will give you a pithy summary.

I once read a viral joke about Ivy League schools and light bulbs that gives you some flavor.

How many Princeton students does it take to change a lightbulb?
> Two—one to mix the martinis and one to call the electrician.

How many Brown students does it take to change a lightbulb?
> Eleven—one to change the lightbulb and 10 to share the experience.

How many Dartmouth students does it take to change a lightbulb?

None—Hanover doesn't have electricity.

How many Cornell students does it take to change a lightbulb?

Two—one to change the lightbulb and one to crack under the pressure.

How many Penn students does it take to change a lightbulb?

Only one—but he gets six credits for it.

How many Columbia students does it take to change a lightbulb?

Seventy-six—one to change the lightbulb, 50 to protest the lightbulb's right to not change, and 25 to hold a counter-protest.

How many Yale students does it take to change a lightbulb?

None—New Haven looks better in the dark.

How many Harvard students does it take to change a lightbulb?

One—he holds the bulb and the world revolves around him.

Okay, not quite university personalities but a funny insight into some of the personas of the universities. In all seriousness, each university has a lot of nuance to it. Here are some insights into the personalities of the Ivy League and Stanford.

Let's start with **Brown.** Brown is known as the least academically restrictive Ivy thanks to their open curriculum, which rejects the traditional core model (see Columbia) so that students might become, as their website touts, the "architects of their own education."

The open curriculum basically means that students don't have any core requirements but can build their own course structure and take some quirky alternatives, for example, the humanities class "The Fugitivity of Slowness, Stillness, and Stasis" and the physics class "The Jazz of Modern Physics."

As a result Brown students are known for being super chill but at the same time very intellectual and passionate. Passionate to the point that one student I heard about walked around campus with his oboe 24/7 (people called him the oboe guy): the oboe chilled on the main green with him, it went to the Rock, Brown's library, when he needed to write papers or read books, and everyone believed that the oboe had a spot by his bed! Another Brown alum friend of mine had a roommate who had a secret cave in the library—apparently she was an art history major and had a pair of pajamas and her tea and honey hidden in a nook! She was there 24/7.

The point here is that Brown is known for being the Ivy where you can be who you are and no one will judge you for it. Brown is known for its supportive community and as a place where students tend to be weird in their own way. It's somewhere between passionate and quirky but highly intellectual in each students' different areas of interest. Unlike other Ivies like Harvard or Princeton, there's no student-to-student competition, and everyone follows their internal compass and time line.

Work hard, play harder—Brown students love life and enjoy it. Students are creative, artistic, and colorful. Many of them voice their ideas freely and the culture is all about sharing, caring, loving, and enjoying one another and life in general. Brown students are interested in many subjects and can connect subjects that might seem irrelevant to many. You can be surprised to see a project from the archeology department that connects French, Math, Biology, and Media Studies in a very logical way and still be presented under the archeology department.

You can graduate with a major you invented and take independent study courses with any professor you feel connected to! I have a friend who did five independent studies at Brown and always said that they could have taken another diploma from that one professor who led all five.

Social justice and liberalism are two prominent attitudes on Brown's Providence campus. Brown is a college for the aspiring artist, the creative type, the postmodern philosopher, or the polyglot. It offers courses such as "Cave Writing"—students can digitally write and paint in a digital cave—or "Writers on Writing"—famous writers visit every class and the class size is very small so the students get to meet and interact with these writers! So in short Brown may not be for everyone, but it's for you then you're bound to enjoy every minute of your more academically flexible, creatively experimental, inclusive college experience.

Cornell is different from the other Ivies, largely because it's pretty big in comparison—about 15,000 undergrads compared to say Princeton's 5,500. This is because it's a private college that also receives some funding from the State of New York and has four state-assigned colleges: Agriculture and Life Sciences, Human Ecology, Industrial and Labor, and Business. Cornell's mission is "any person, any study."

Cornell has a unique school offering in the form of the School of Hotel Administration, the first four-year institution in hotel administration in the US (and also in the world). The 150 or so students who study there are known as the *hotelies* and supposedly you can pick them a mile away because they dress more formally around campus. The school is also very self-contained with almost all classes taking place inside the hotel school and in the Statler Hotel—which is an upscale, entirely student-run hotel right opposite of the Johnson School of Business. Hotelies dine in their own cafeteria and host their own social gatherings.

That said, the hotelies are obviously in the minority and given Cornell's size, students from different colleges and majors interact fluidly. It's not uncommon for students to cross-register for classes in other colleges and for students and faculty in different colleges to collaborate on research projects. Even though the coursework at Cornell is quite intense, students do have a full and balanced education and social life.

One thing Cornell does have a reputation for is a higher student suicide rate than other colleges driven by the fact that there have been some historical clusters of suicides at the bridges spanning the gorges that are carved into the Ithaca landscape. Although Cornell does not in fact have an above-average suicide rate compared to other colleges, these sorts of stories make for dramatic media fodder. That said, it is true that Cornell school is remote, and the winters are long, and because the campus is very spread out, students find themselves trekking up and down the hilly paths constantly, battling the snow simply to get to class, which can certainly make things tough in the colder months. But Cornell is also known as the school with the most down-to-earth students who are serious about learning but more collaborative than some of their Ivy compatriots.

On the social side, Greek life is big at Cornell with one-third of the students belonging to a fraternity or sorority. Students who are not involved in Greek life find themselves gravitating toward other social groups on campus. This is in contrast to bustling city schools in New York City or Boston, where students have opportunities to be social beyond the confines of the university. If you're an outdoor person, Ithaca is pretty hard to beat—hiking trails, state parks, waterfalls, lakes. Many students pick up one or two new sports, from sailing or kayaking, horseback riding or cross country running, during their time at Cornell.

Finally, Cornelians have a reputation for having an a capella group singing under every arch—so they are up there in the Ivy a capella cliche-feeding stakes—but probably not as high up as Yale.

Although **Columbia** exists in the same state as Cornell—they may as well be on different planets. One of Columbia's biggest draw cards, and part of the reason why its admit rate is so low, is its location in New York City. This in itself shapes the school's culture and personality.

First its proximity to Wall Street, banks, consultancy firms, and other financial institutions means that these top companies are frequently holding recruitment events on campus. There are ample opportunities for students to network and get recruitment coaching. Finance and economics are among the most popular majors among Columbia students. Similarly, Columbia's location provides students with access to diplomats and multilateral institutions. Every year the United National General Assembly and the university organize "Global Leaders Week," where presidents, prime ministers, and diplomats are invited to campus to meet and speak with students.

The school is also famous for its core curriculum (the anti-Brown), which means all students have to undertake certain courses in certain areas, which has resulted in it being a great place to excel in everything from finance and economics to the social sciences. Its professors are some of the world's leading thinkers in anthropology; Middle Eastern and African studies; Indigenous studies, post-Colonial thought; women's, gender, and sexuality studies; and ethnicity and race studies. It's hall of fame include figures such as Edward Said, Gayatri Spivak, Lila Abu-Lughod, and Rashid Khalidi.

Harking back to my light bulb joke, Columbia has the reputation of being the "activist Ivy." A big portion of

Columbians have very progressive values on all sorts of issues from environmentalism to mass incarceration, land occupation, indigenous rights, LGBTQ rights, and more. The university has been a sight of nationally famous protests and sit-ins, and represents the forceful role young people have played in transforming and evolving institutions. Recently, sit-ins organized by Columbia Divest led to the university pledging to divest from companies profiting from mass incarceration.

On the social front, Columbia student life is not as concentrated within the campus gates as it might be in other Ivies. The social life of students is extended throughout New York City itself. Columbia students enjoy theatre, the great many New York museums (which they get free access to), NYC nightlife, restaurants, and parks just as much, if not more, than campus events. This is a good balance to what is also an intensely rigorous academic institution. Most courses are graded on a curve, resulting in Columbia having a reputation for harboring a constantly academically competitive atmosphere.

If you wanted to pick the Ivy that was the absolute antithesis of Columbia—at least when it comes to location— you would trek way up north to **Dartmouth** in Hanover, New Hampshire. From the air Hanover looks like a rectangle cut-out in a sea of dark green trees.

Dartmouth is the smallest Ivy with only 4,500 undergrads and Hanover really is the quintessential college town, which can mean isolationist for some students who prefer the rigor of New York or Boston or heaven for some who crave a uniquely inclusive experience.

If you choose Dartmouth over say, Harvard or Columbia, then good for you, as it probably means you'll thrive in a place where you and your peers figure out how to make stuff happen rather than letting the location do it for you.

Dartmouth is unusual as it's the only Ivy with a "D-Plan," which means you can opt to take your classes over the summer and choose another semester to take off. Any college student will tell you that the competition for summer internships is fierce—so Dartmouth introduced the D-Plan so their students could land top internships away from the June to August hustle.

Academically there is a sense of collaboration with former students saying the undergrad focus means more time with top professors, and the small student population means greater collaboration where the pressure comes from performing at your best over nailing a top grade. Academically the school has a reputation for collaboration—which may be explained by the remoteness of the location but also by the tendency for Dartmouth students to give their professors rigorous feedback in the positive or the negative. It's said the faculty take all this commentary into account, which leads to a sense of humility and equality on campus, and may line up with the belief that Dartmouth students walk to the beat of their own drum.

Dartmouth students are also less inclined to be caught up in appearances and say what they want to say, not what others expect them to.

On the cultural front Dartmouth students pride themselves on doing everything "hard"—studying, partying, or undertaking a 54-mile hike to the top of Mount Moosilauke, which you're encouraged to complete in 24 hours. This may explain why the school has produced a number of Olympians in sports such as skiing and cross country running. Socially Greek Life is big and to a degree competes with the (administration's) push to base social life around the house system.

The **University of Pennsylvania** is very popular among our students. Ninety-nine of our students have received UPenn offers so far and the culture is quite distinctive.

First, it is the most pre-professional of any of the Ivy League schools. *Pre-professional* means that students are very focused on pursuing a pathway that helps them land a job, usually a well-paying job on Wall Street or in management consulting. A lot of universities will try to throw shade at places that are pre-professional because they argue that higher education is supposed to primarily teach you how to think and expose you to new concepts and academic exploration. I appreciate the argument, but I find this to be slightly arrogant and a bit luxurious.

Let me explain. University is a huge investment. Getting into an Ivy League school requires so much disciplined persistence and it doesn't just happen randomly. Very few students would pursue the same types of activities and types of competitions as they do if the US college application process didn't exist. Therefore, students are happy to optimize to boost their odds of getting into a top college. Is it surprising then that they generally love universities that are super focused on making sure they land their dream jobs? I embrace pre-professional-focused environments because ultimately that aligns to what the typical student is looking for.

The University of Pennsylvania is home to Wharton, the Wall Street factory. At Harvard, it is hard to find a finance or accounting class. You need to cross-register at MIT to take accounting. You have to walk across the Charles River to Harvard Business School to find some of the cross-registered business classes if you want to pursue strategy or entrepreneurship classes. The economics department generally tries to avoid teaching financial modeling, valuation analysis, and some of the other tools used on Wall Street on a daily basis. Wharton takes the opposite approach. It equips students with a weapons arsenal of skills—finance, modeling, marketing, strategy, leadership, human resources, product management.

Wharton is incredibly focused on making sure that its graduates are extremely well trained to win the most-sought-after jobs on Wall Street—and the school relishes their reputation for accomplishing this. A number of the most elite private equity firms such as Silver Lake have reputations for only hiring from a very narrow set of undergraduate institutions. Wharton is a favorite. Similarly, if you look at top hedge funds like Elliot Management or Tiger Global, you will often see many of the analysts have Wharton undergraduate degrees.

What does this mean for culture?

If you want to go to UPenn and discover your soul talking philosophically about alternative market structures, you probably aren't in the right place. At UPenn, expect a lot of conversation to be about what internships you have landed, what classes you are taking, and that student who just landed the awesome opportunity at a private equity fund. People are competitive at UPenn and students feel this. There is strong pressure on people to pursue a traditionally successful career, especially at Wharton. This significant pressure results in a need for stress release!

This may then explain why UPenn is regarded as the Ivy League school with the best parties. It often tops lists for the biggest party school in the US. In my orientation at UPenn as a prospective student, I remember walking inside a fraternity for the very first time (outside of watching these things on *American Pie*). I was a little star-struck because the fraternity I visited was used in the set of *Transformers: Revenge of the Fallen*, which at the time was one of my all-time favorite movies.

Stanford has a legendary reputation and for good reason. Stanford and Silicon Valley are inextricably linked. When I was pursuing my MBA at Stanford, Tyra Banks came in for a class on personal brand management, Eric

Schmidt (CEO of Google) came in to teach entrepreneurship and venture capital, Evan Spiegel (Founder of Snapchat) came in to guest lecture a class on product and this doesn't even include the rotating door of guest speakers (Hillary Clinton fresh off her stinging 2016 loss was a fascinating one!).

Being so close to Silicon Valley, Stanford is the undergraduate college of choice for hiring for many of the elite venture capital funds, private equity funds, and other West Coast firms. The most popular major at Stanford is computer science and the coolest thing to do on campus is to create your own company (or potentially drop out and create your own company but I am negative on dropping out). This culture of entrepreneurship breeds broad fascination in Stanford students with many different industries as they hunt for opportunities to launch the next big tech unicorn.

At Stanford, at peak lunch times you need to be careful to not be a motor vehicle fatality because of the hordes of bicycles zooming in every direction. Stanford students value health and fitness and generally like to cycle a lot given the expansive campus and put a lot of focus on personal fitness, the gym, and exercise. I don't mind a late night bag of chocolate M&Ms as long as they aren't peanut flavored. Good luck finding them in a Stanford vending machine! I had to choke my way through Caesar salads and exotic variants of iced tea from the health-conscious vending machines by my dorm.

A last point on Stanford—it has a bit of a culture of wrapping things in a smile. There is a metaphor of a duck on water often used to describe Stanford students. On the surface, the duck looks calm, relaxed, and chilled out. Under the water, their legs are frantically beating to keep moving forwards and stay up. In some schools, the culture is to share your miseries and complain about your endless homework. Stanford tends to be the opposite.

Yale is often regarded as the happiest Ivy. I don't deny it. At Yale Bulldog Days, the pre-frosh event for recent admits, you do feel a little spellbound by the optimistic euphoria around the place. Yale also has one of the most thriving LGBTQ+ communities of any of the Ivy League schools. It is a supportive, happy environment that lacks some of the competitive sharp edges of a place like Wharton. It has a strong intellectual culture and a real strength in the humanities, social sciences, debating, government, and public policy. It is no surprise that Yale is home to the best law school in the US.

Yale also has a fantastic underground network of tunnels that are very reminiscent of Hogwarts or a spy movie. To escape the cold winters, you can shimmy from house to house and visit your classmates, play basketball underground or even munch some snacks in a "buttery," a kind of underground bar that many of the colleges have. There's also a bar close to campus called "Toads," and on Wednesday "Woads" is only open to Yalies.

Yale is probably most famous for its secret societies that students get tapped for. The most famous is the Skull & Bones society but there is also one called Wolf's Head, which was founded by a student who was really into Egyptology (to compete against Skull & Bones). Beyond that, there are the cliches that are there for a reason—like Yale's obsession with a capella (the Yale Wiffenpoofs have been known—pre-COVID—to do world tours and draw a pretty decent global crowd), the green quadrangles, and the passion for a well-rounded liberal arts education, even though a decent number of Yalies end up going into finance.

Academically—which may also align with the happiest Ivy reputation—there's the general consensus that grades are slightly inflated at Yale compared to the other Ivies and professors are pretty generous with extensions.

In contrast to their Bull Dog rivals, at **Princeton,** students pride themselves on attending what they consider to be the most academically rigorous Ivy League School. You'll often overhear students dismissing Harvard as "easy," complaining that the students at the most famed Ivy institution don't suffer from the dreaded "grade deflation." Although this phenomenon was supposedly remedied several years ago, many students maintain its lingering legacy, which wreaks havoc on Princetonians' grades. You'll often find students competing on the basis of who has received the least amount of sleep the previous night.

Although Princeton is not as pre-professional as perhaps UPenn, most students feel the pressure to divert their academic careers toward one of the "trinity": tech, consulting, and finance. Accordingly, most students find themselves majoring in computer science, public and international affairs, or economics. For those who are eager to pursue a career in engineering, these students opt for a bachelor's in science and engineering (BSE), although, most eschew the intensity and specialization of a BSE degree in favor of a bachelor's in arts (BA).

Princeton is perhaps most often characterized as the home of the trust fund babies. Perhaps one of the most popular rumors of the past few years was that Jeff Bezos's son had joined the freshman cohort under a different name to protect his privacy. Such a reputation has often been a source of criticism for Princeton. Last year's reckoning in terms of the Black Lives Matter movement shed light on Princeton's ties with racism, prompting it to remove Woodrow Wilson's name from the school. Further concern was raised when many anecdotes of students experiencing racism, shared on the "Black Ivy Stories" Instagram account, were attributed to Princeton. However, in recent years Princeton has made increasing efforts to diversify its student body and provide greater opportunities for low-income, first-generation students.

Many students of Princeton live by the motto "work hard, play hard." Students let off steam by heading to "the street," which is literally a street just off campus lined with "eating clubs." These clubs are the heart of social activity on campus, given Greek life is not allowed (there are, however, a handful of sororities and fraternities that nonetheless operate out of Princeton). Students have the option to join an eating club in the spring of their sophomore year. Although some eating clubs are "sign-in," meaning they accept all who wish to join, many are "bicker." The bicker process often involves sophomores engaging in a menagerie of social events and having one-on-one conversations with club members, after which members of the club decide who makes the cut and who will be "hosed." Although the process is only three days long, the prospect of being hosed places students under pressure to increase their chances of acceptance, with many sophomores attempting to forge connections beforehand to shore up their rates of success.

Harvard feels like it runs on ambition. One of the things I found to be surprising is that Harvard never seemed so competitive and cut-throat between students. It felt like everyone was racing to achieve their ambitions, pushing themself in their own domains, but people largely were unified by their ambition and desire for personal growth as opposed to pulled apart by it. Harvard doesn't have as much of an entrepreneurial culture as a place like Stanford or Wharton but still has a reasonable presence of aspiring founders. In recent years, incredible companies like Stripe and Facebook have emerged from Harvard students.

Many Harvard undergraduates are fascinated by politics, government, and aspire to go into public service in some capacity. As mentioned, the most popular major at

Harvard is economics, which tends to be a nice catch-all for aspiring public policymakers, financiers, people looking for a relatively relaxed major, and a whole spectrum of other niches. Computer science is growing, partially because of the success of David Malan's CS50, which has become an internet phenomenon teaching undergraduate students computer science with no prerequisites. The sheer resources of the institution enable it to offer a wide variety of well-resourced faculty and niche majors from statistics to folklore and mythology to philosophy with considerable depth in course offering.

It feels like Harvard and many of these colleges can create what I describe as "parallel realities." Two students could both go to Harvard and have wildly different experiences. I roomed with the same awesome group of roommates for three years and across our group we had people concentrating in biomedical engineering, physics, sociology, government, applied mathematics-economics, economics, psychology, and history. We almost had no extracurriculars in common. We often were in different parts of the campuses with different professors, different career aspirations, and differing challenges. Although we were all Harvard undergrads, our realities varied enormously. This is part of the beauty of the liberal arts system and one of the magical aspects of the larger universities that can resource a spectrum of majors successfully.

So how do you detect the personalities of your institution? On the surface, a lot of these universities on the internet look very similar. To really get to know an institution, you need to speak with at least five different people from it and ask them to describe what they like and don't like about it (something we have done on our viral "Big Questions" series on YouTube under Crimson Education).

You want to understand what the food is like, how competitive the environment is, how pre-professional it is, what career paths, what majors and what extracurricular activities are possible. You want to know about the weather (Boston winters were so brutal and I only realized just how brutal they were after I went to Stanford and experienced California weather). You also want to know about the support for international students and if many students from your country or state have been there.

Try and get people to open up and be real with you about their experiences. Most people will love their university but you are trying to dig into the nuance to see what is right for you. Some of the personality nuances aren't so important to understand during the application process but when you are choosing between a couple of final options, you want to make a lot of effort to understand these nuances.

Chapter 19

For Parents Only!

For most of our adventure throughout *ACCEPTED!* I've largely focused on speaking to the students. In my experience, the students who ultimately gain admission to these top universities generally (with very few notable exceptions) have strong intrinsic motivation. They are competitive, they want to do well, and they recognize the role that university will have in catalyzing their career.

Not every student starts this way, but everyone who ends up thriving throughout high school tends to be defined by these traits. But, behind every successful student is usually a devoted parent (or two). Behind them are often some devoted grandparents. The parent's role in helping the child on this journey is absolutely fundamental.

I am not a parent (yet) and although I would love to be in the future, I will give you my perspective on what you need to know as a parent. My perspective comes from getting to know thousands of parents of different ethnicities and socioeconomic backgrounds all over the world from Russia to China to Korea to the US to Australia to New Zealand in action, and the results of their parenting styles and approaches.

One of life's peculiar ironies is that there are few decisions in life that have such profound consequences as having a child. When parents decide intentionally or unintentionally to conceive a child, they are signing up for an incredibly high commitment that straddles at least 18 years and beyond.

Having a child and growing a family is ultimately what we are wired to do genetically to continue humanity's march forwards. I would challenge you as a prospective parent to go in wide-eyed with your approach and philosophy to having your baby. Do you want them to be set up for success on the world stage? How much time do you really have to support them? Do you have the emotional bandwidth and family stability to support their development?

I am not the type of person (and even when I am a parent I suspect that this will not change) to tell you that everyone who has a baby spends a great deal of time getting their head around what is going on and trying to figure out what to do next. On the contrary, I see massive differences in the caliber of parenting from family to family, the quality of relationships they have at home, and the subsequent impact on the child. I won't wax lyrical about these nuances but will focus on giving you some practical observations and advice.

First, a story. All around the world, Crimson runs events in which prospective students and parents come along to hear about how they can tackle the education journey ahead. In our events in New Zealand in a room of 100, we will often see 70 kids, 20 mums, and 10 dads.

For events in Korea, guess what the room looks like?

In a room of 100, there are usually 99 mums and 1 dad (good on this guy).

Korean mums work in packs researching the best education providers and share notes and referrals within tight-knit circles of friends. A term has emerged—a "pig mum"—referring to one who is fully immersed in organizing, scheduling, and managing their child's education process from primary to secondary school to planning for their higher education. I don't know why *pig* is in the name but the intensity and focus of the parents in these rooms are palpable.

In many of the Asian cultures across Japan, China, and Korea, the gender responsibilities within the family are very explicitly defined. The mother often is charged with making sure the child thrives in their education and often steps back from work (although this trend is changing now) to commit, full-time, to helping their child optimize their education journey.

I meet many mothers in these countries who have a truly encyclopedia-like knowledge of the college admissions process, different curriculum, different local competitions, and how competitive they are, as well as an exhaustive knowledge of the strengths and weaknesses of different education providers. These families naturally love Crimson because we understand them and make their mission substantially easier and more effective.

It is fascinating to observe in Western economies the extreme cultural divide concerning education. Asian families are generally happy to spend a substantially higher (think 10 times) proportion of their household income on education services and support for their children. They don't naturally assume that spending money on cars, food, vacations, or clothing items takes priority over their child's education. I see families who spend materially all of their disposable savings on their child's education—like my cofounder Fangzhou. His family grew up in Xi'an, China. They worked very modest jobs and spent nearly their entire savings to send Fangzhou to New Zealand for three years of his high school education in the hope of giving him a better future.

Fangzhou arrived in New Zealand not speaking much English at the age of 15. He had seen that his parents had sacrificed virtually everything for him and he landed in New Zealand with a burning mission to be successful.

To help pay for his textbooks, he worked at a Chinese restaurant that paid him $8/hour. He would walk (because he had no car and the bus lines weren't so good) almost one hour to work for two to three hours and then he would walk back home. He didn't know anyone in New Zealand and literally couldn't speak the language.

He trained himself in English by watching all kinds of Western movies with various subtitles, invested his money from his restaurant work to get the best textbooks and pay for examination entry fees. Fast-forward three years, Fangzhou was Dux (Valedictorian) of the biggest school in New Zealand, Rangitoto College.

He went on to sit the competitive NZQA Scholarship exams and became the first international student in the history of New Zealand (and only to this day) to win an NZQA Premier Scholar awarded by then–New Zealand Prime Minister Sir John Key (who now sits on our advisory board).

I met Fangzhou because he reached out to me as one of our very first students. I was at Harvard at the time and to look more professional during the consultation, I swung my desk around so it didn't look like a dorm room so my back was against the wall. On the wall, I had a New Zealand flag.

Fangzhou wanted help securing a full scholarship to a top university. He had a couple of thousands in savings and paid an hourly rate to work with me on his applications to various schools. I didn't realize at the time, but each hour he purchased with me was about five hours of his Chinese takeaway shop earnings. He was a man on a mission.

He won a full scholarship to Australian National University, Australia's highest-ranked university according to QS World University Rankings. After getting in, he joined Sharndre—my other cofounder—and me. Fangzhou has gone on to complete a master's in management science and engineering at Stanford University. He has completed a Schwarzman Scholarship at Tsinghua University. More important, he has helped me build Crimson from a dorm room start-up to a global organization for which I will be eternally grateful.

I was very lucky in that my mum worked very hard with me every spare moment of every day—and perhaps it was this, combined with Fangzhou's awe-inspiring story, that made me realize that the grit and determination that defines a significant proportion of Chinese students and their families can cross cultures.

So what do I recommend to support your child?

First, your child generally has no idea about what they like up until the age of around 10 to 12. As a result, you as the parent can play a very active role in helping them discover their strengths by curating a range of activities to expose them to. Mandarin? Computer science? Music? Sports? Debating and theatre? Robotics? Community service? Don't passively assume your child will wake up one day and discover their magic interest. My mother systematically exposed me to a wide variety of activities and subjects so I could figure out my strengths and weaknesses.

Second, remember that very few high fliers who are successful early in life were magically born with these abilities. Tiger Woods didn't get out of bed and decided to start obsessively swinging his golf club. His father drilled him with practice, training, and structure to push him to build these skills. Now, I'm not necessarily advocating for this, but exceptional outliers don't magically arise. Most of the high-flying academic students I meet had parents who exposed them to rigorous mathematics and english preparation very early in their lives, before they knew anything better.

If parents normalize regular tutoring, academic support, reading, and high academic standards, the child will absorb the knowledge like osmosis before they have any real free will on the matter. I loved academics but I wasn't going to magically find mathematics and english tutors, buy my own books, or study for my exams by myself. My mum sat with me basically each week day and every weekend until I was 10 or 11 helping me to foster strong academic skills.

Third, parent-student-teacher alignment is crucial. One of the key findings from my recent DPhil work at Oxford was that it is critical that all education stakeholders are aligned. Parents often have a warped or nonexistent sense of their child's performance, skills, and interests. When the student's perception of their skills deviates from reality and/or the parent's perception of their child deviates from reality, it creates all kinds of problems. I've seen kids who get an arrogant complex because they are fed a narrative that they are so smart by their parents only to test them and realize they have big gaps. I see families fighting sometimes because the child and the parents have different sets of ambitions or expectations. The most effective students generally have a parent or two behind them who have a clear sense of their ability, what they are going through, and what their ambitions are, and when that is the case they can act as an emotional support pillar as opposed to a source of conflict and pressure.

Fourth, lead by example. Every day I woke up and I saw my mum's degrees on the wall of my bedroom. At a time when university education was free in New Zealand, she pursued a law degree, commerce degree, MBA, and chartered accounting proficiency. My mum would work incredibly hard and diligently to grow her business, look after my grandparents and me, and always made time to help me whenever I needed it.

I grew up with a cultural norm that you get things in life through relentless hard work, a competitive will to win, and by thriving in formal education structures. My mum probably told me these things over the years, but I mainly got the message by soaking it up—by simply being her son. Children are smart and they are like sponges—they are influenced in good ways and in bad ways by their parents. How could I chill and take school easily when I saw how hard my mother worked to give me the set of opportunities I had? I took every hour of tutoring as a precious gift because I knew I was putting some financial pressure on her, and I was going to move heaven and earth to make sure it was worth it.

Fifth, create a high-trust culture with your child. I always grew up feeling I could tell my mum anything and she would be there for me. When I was in trouble, I would tell her. My mother never stopped me going to parties, dating girls, buying Halo (an R-16 video game) years before I hit the magic age of 16, or watching *American Pie* movies with my friends at sleepovers in my tweens.

She never really told me to not drink alcohol or take drugs. She didn't have to. She had wired me with many of her own values. She didn't drink alcohol, she took her career seriously, and poured so much love and effort into me that I just wasn't going to do too many dumb things because I always felt supported and trusted. I could feel her belief in me every day and that led me to make better decisions than many of my peers, who had strict rules in place but often would go around them in any case and spiral into challenging situations. Nurture an open dialogue so your child can feel as though they can tell you things in an unfiltered way—things they probably can't trust anyone else with.

Finally, celebrate your child's hobbies and passions in all areas. Nurturing intrinsic passion is critical because it becomes very hard to achieve results with your child through a purely pressure-based, extrinsic motivation incentive system. My mum took me to Yu-Gi-Oh tournaments (with my friends like Alvis Lee and Sean Kim) that required long multi-hour road trips.

She taxied me to Warhammer stores on weeknights so I could play Warhammer 40k, a tabletop strategy game. She would let me invite ridiculous numbers of friends to play paintball for five years of birthday parties in a row. No one becomes good at anything unless they have a kind of thrilling, obsessive intensity. Let them find passions that rivet them, even if they appear irrelevant, because as long as you are setting them up for academic success, some of that obsessive passion is likely to manifest in certain academic fields.

Specifically in the college application process try to do these things:

- Discuss early (ages 12–13) the importance of aiming high for college applications and what this means for their future so they are operating in a world where the expectation is that they go to a good college and will take the preparation process for this seriously.

- Try and expose your child to new environments, new challenges, and potential adversity actively. From bungee jumping to being obliterated by paintballs to failing at basketball to experiencing different cultural backgrounds. The more life experiences your child has had, the more self-aware they will become (and the more fertile essay topics there will be!).
- Don't say things like "wherever you end up is okay." If your child is taking the process seriously, it is far more thrilling to have the parents come along for the journey, be thinking strategically with the child, and be encouraging the child to think big. Comments like this can just undermine your child's ambition subconsciously. It is okay to be ambitious! Normalize ambition and achievement in your family.
- Don't try to remove all pressure from your child's life as they embark on the gauntlet of college admissions. When they become an adult, you can't shield them from all of the pressures of life. Instead, be there for your child when they fail (as my mum did after I failed in every single tennis tournament I competed in for almost five years). Help them to establish pressure management techniques (like consistent exercise, strong sleep, mentorship, and academic support), as opposed to hiding from the reality that this is a somewhat stressful process.
- Take part in the essay brainstorming sessions! You will have fascinating insights into your child that they may not have observed or realized. Don't dominate the process but be a willing contributor of ideas for things like the Common Application essays.
- Set the expectation that a portion of every school holiday will be used for extension academic and extracurricular work. I used some of my holidays to do

training for math exams, completed Duke of Edinburgh hikes in the woods, and self-studied subjects. Most of the ambitious students I see are used to doing activities that drive personal growth every holiday from a young age. A balance between total holidays and relaxation and using the time for structured growth is important to build your college profile and normalize the pursuit of achievement.

- Don't set your child's goals for them. Prompt them to set their own. Don't tell your kid to aim for Harvard. Explain how universities work and the benefits of stronger institutions and get them to do their own research and tell you where they want to aim for. Goals set by other people feel like uninspiring homework. It is critical that as soon as possible, the student is the one setting their most ambitious goals.

- Stay very close to your child's academics. I have seen some hands-off parenting styles work occasionally, but not very often. In general, the most successful kids have some of the most engaged parents. If you plot contact hours between the children and their parents in which they discuss education-related matters against the success of the child, there seems to be a strong relationship from what I have observed so far. If you, as the parent, can't tell me what your child's curriculum is, when their next set of exams are roughly, what their main extracurriculars are, or vaguely what their upcoming goals for the year are, you probably aren't close enough to their academic journey.

- Don't be cheap. My mind is blown sometimes when meeting certain parents. I have met families who buy plastic surgery, carry fancy designer handbags, live in sprawling houses, and take expensive vacations. When it comes down to writing a small cheque for some additional support for their child, they don't want to pay it. In a particular example that comes to mind, the child could have ended up at an undergraduate business school like Wharton but the parents wanted to avoid a bit of out-of-pocket expenses, told the child that local options were fine, and now he is at a local university and really struggling to break into the investing industry. If Fangzhou's parents are willing to invest all their disposable income into his education, you should be willing to invest a reasonable amount into your child's education. This doesn't require investing in education like families do in China or Korea, but you should expect that the generic education system is not going to cater to all the personalized needs of your child. Most of the students I see that end up at top institutions in the US from a wide variety of socioeconomic backgrounds typically had a lot of tutoring and other educational investment in them over several years. It is very hard to get to the US Open playing tennis without a top tennis coach. Academics are no different.

- Don't force career pathways onto your child. I meet some families who are obsessed with their child being a doctor because of the secure salary and prestige. Being a doctor and not liking it is utterly depressing (and I have seen this happen many times). Make sure they have rigorous academic foundations, are exposed to a wide variety of potential interests to be able to make informed decisions and cheer them on as they go through this self-discovery process. You can brainwash your child up until the age of about 12 but the strategy runs out of steam in the high school years and can end badly. Remember that virtually all the students I have trained that ended up at these top universities tend to have strong intrinsic motivation by high school.

When it comes to academics, I have great respect for China, India, and Korea. Consider that in New Zealand only 15% of the country come from an Asian background yet about 70% of the admits to the Ivy League schools tend to come from an Asian background. These students don't outperform because they have a magically higher IQ. They actually often face structural disadvantages in the application process. One of the major reasons these segments outperform by so much is because of the massive difference in parenting styles, attitude toward academic success, and their general willingness to invest in their children's education.

As a parent, soak up the best characteristics of Western and Eastern parenting and don't always take the path most trodden or of least resistance.

My mum was my strongest ally, biggest cheerleader, best pillar of emotional support and my most inspiring role model. Try and foster this relationship with your child and you will see the results of the greatest gift you can give them—a good education—and the lifelong benefits of being a parent to a child who reached their goals thanks to your dedication, love, and support.

Epilogue

I promised you secrets of gaining admission into the world's best universities. I didn't muck you around. You've learned a lot:

1. Take as many subjects as possible. Class spam, subject to getting strong grades, continues to be highly effective.
2. Use Early Decision to boost your odds but be strategic about the school you apply to. You only get one shot.

    You won't have your future all figured out. I didn't. But in your application, you will tell a persuasive narrative as to what you want to achieve in the future. "Undecided" is uninspiring.
3. You will analyze the results/effort ratio of all your activities and eliminate the time wasters and double down on your competitive niche once you find it.
4. You won't wait around to be given a leadership role. You will create one yourself and launch your own initiative.
5. You will build strong relationships with your teachers so they are closely involved in your extracurriculars and can endorse the impact of your leadership.
6. If you can, you will land holy grail extracurriculars: Olympiad medals, RSI admissions, INTEL Science Fair awards, or more.

7. You will treat "optional" as "compulsory."
8. You'll seriously consider some of the unique dual degrees that may be a path less trodden but could be perfect for you.
9. You will use your summers effectively and choose programs that really move the dial of your application.
10. You'll delicately manage your mental health and balance the pressure of the process sustainably.
11. You will make sure you have strong academic fundamentals, even if you are an all-star athlete.
12. You will use the "wisdom of the crowd" and a college's personality to evaluate where you want to go more effectively and be shameless about it. This is your future!

There are hacks, there are strategies, there are tactics, and they can all incrementally help. Generally, however, the student with the best results tends to be the hardest working. The Dux or Valedictorian, more often than not, studied for more hours than anybody else. I didn't get into all the universities I have by taking it easy and neither did our students who have received 370+ offers to the Ivy League. They ran at this process with the competitive intensity that a professional athlete might pursue in a competition. You need to work hard. You need to push yourself and keep pushing yourself. Why?

It is far easier to make it your mission to thrive in high school, get into a brilliant university, then ride the benefits of that degree and training in the job market and your career than to chill, take it easy, and then try and amplify your career down the line. Certain industries such as management consulting, investment banking, venture capital, and technology are virtually impossible to get into from most standard academic backgrounds. At Stanford Business School's MBA program, there were 40 kids from Harvard undergrad, 35 kids from Stanford undergrad, and one kid from University of Auckland. That student was incredibly smart, had a near perfect GPA in chemical engineering, and was very talented. Many more students at his university would have had the potential to perform well in a Stanford MBA class, but it is just so much harder to get in from a typical program than from a leading undergraduate university. If you are reading this in high school, trust me—it is worth the hard work now. I've seen time and time again across thousands of students how these higher education institutions can give you the kind of jump-start, space-like propulsion that will open doors you never dreamed possible.

Don't let people tell you that you can do your undergraduate degree anywhere and get more serious for postgrad. Don't let people tell you about how Mark Zuckerberg and Bill Gates (both admitted to Harvard) dropped out so you can too (maybe, but only after you get into Harvard). These references sound helpful but have sinister implications that high school doesn't matter. High school is high stakes. It is empowering when you see reality for what it is, you embrace it, and you run at it with everything you've got.

I see students who didn't try their best in high school, didn't get into the universities they wanted, and it can disengage them from really trying for years and years. Whether you have realized your career direction or not, don't stress. I changed my mind many times throughout high school and many more times throughout college.

This doesn't stop you pushing your academics and extracurriculars and challenging yourself across a wide variety of areas.

Most people who get into these leading universities don't do it by accident. They think strategically about all their activities, academics, recommendation letters, leadership initiatives, personal statements, and approach to high school with a powerful mix of competitiveness, ambition, strategic planning, and pragmatism. You can't go through high school and do whatever you like. Any admissions officer who tells you this is kidding themselves. The application process necessitates that you think several years ahead and approach this journey with precision.

Some people will look at you funny as you launch your next club or mention you are taking an AP exam already or wonder why you do so many competitions. I finished high school almost 10 years ago to this day, and after studying at Harvard, Stanford, Oxford, Yale, working on Wall Street and building Crimson all over the world, no one asks me anymore why I did all the things I did in high school.

Ignore the haters. Ignore the forces that pull you toward average. Ignore the constraints of your institution. Ignore your age. There should be nothing that limits your ambition. Be proud that you want to get into one of these top universities. Be proud of your academic curiosity.

If you haven't yet found a community behind you that champions your passion, don't worry. Once you land at one of these institutions, once you are accepted, you will. Landing at these colleges is a kind of cathartic experience. You realize you weren't alone. There are thousands of students just like you all over the US and all over the world who take their future as seriously as you do.

- Five honors
- 10 extracurriculars
- Class rank
- Academic transcript
- Standardized tests
- Additional college/university courses
- Intended career pathway
- Highest education intended

- Family background
- Citizenship status
- Additional information
- Application essays

These are seemingly simple requirements of the US application process but behind them applicants put in thousands of hours of work over their education journey to being the best version of themselves they can be. Relish in the journey.

You will grow enormously throughout the process. You will learn how to manage your time. You will learn how to respond under pressure. You will learn how to deal with competition. You will learn awesome new material and discover new subjects. You will have sleepless nights. You will have huge wins. You will have painful losses. You will build like-minded friendships. You will learn more about the world's most pressing social issues. You will become a leader.

You will be ACCEPTED!

Appendix: Bonus Round

The *Accepted!* Strategy in Action: A Detailed Look at the Applications of Five Students Who Were Admitted to the Best Universities in the US

For the most astute students out there, here is a behind the scenes look at five successful applicants who gained admission into the world's top universities by applying the principles explored in this book. Here are our secrets one more time:

1. Take as many subjects as possible. Class spam, subject to getting strong grades, continues to be highly effective.
2. Use Early Decision to boost your odds but be strategic about the school you apply for. You only get one shot.
3. You won't have your future all figured out. I didn't. But in your application, you will tell a persuasive narrative as to what you want to achieve in the future. "Undecided" is uninspiring.
4. You will analyze the results/effort ratio of all your activities and eliminate the time wasters and double down on your competitive niche once you find it.

5. You won't wait around to be given a leadership role. You will create one yourself and launch your own initiative.
6. You will build strong relationships with your teachers so they are closely involved in your extracurriculars and can endorse the impact of your leadership.
7. If you can, you will land holy grail extracurriculars: Olympiad medals, RSI admissions, INTEL Science Fair awards, or more.
8. You will treat "optional" as "compulsory."
9. You'll seriously consider some of the unique dual degrees that may be a path less trodden but could be perfect for you.
10. You will use your summers effectively and choose programs that really move the dial of your application.
11. You'll delicately manage your mental health and balance the pressure of the process sustainably.
12. You will make sure you have strong academic fundamentals, even if you are an all-star athlete.
13. You will use the "wisdom of the crowd" and a college's personality to evaluate where you want to go more effectively and be shameless about it. This is your future!

Case Study 1 The Harvard Slam Dunk: Student Government Lead and 15 APs

This student was admitted into Harvard, Columbia, Cornell, Duke, Emory, Johns Hopkins, the University of Pennsylvania, Rice University, and more.

Here is a summary of her Common App profile:

Curriculum and Details	Score
SAT	Did not sit due to Covid
SAT Subject Tests	Did not sit due to Covid

AP Subject Tests:
  Physics C Mechanics
  Chemistry
  Economics:
    Microeconomics
  Economics:
    Macroeconomics
  English Literature &
    Composition
  Statistics
  Biology
  English Language &
    Composition
  Government & Politics:
    Comparative
  United States History
  Calculus BC
  Calculus AB
  Environmental Science
  World History
  Human Geography
	
	5
	5
	5
	
	4
	
	5
	5
	5
	4
	5

(continued)

(*continued*)

Honors, Awards, and Achievements

Details
National Advanced Placement Scholar
College Board National Rural and Small Town Recognition Program Winner
Questbridge College Prep Scholar
National Association for the Advancement of Colored People Thomas Jackson Community Service Award
Georgia Governor's Honors Program Social Studies

Latin Honors:
    Three-time National Latin Exam Perfect Scorer
    Georgia Junior Classical League Latin History/Culture 2 Exam 1st Prize
    Georgia Junior Classical League Certamen Champion
    Georgia Latin Sight Reading Competition summa cum laude

Nonacademic Honors:
    Carnegie Hall Debut as Concertmaster at National Orchestra and Band Festival
    Georgia All-State Full Orchestra First Violin

(continued)

Activities/Extracurriculars

Activity	Description
Journalism/ Publication	Int'l & Mag. Director, Editor-in-Chief; Writer, Femme for Ed; Int'l Youth STEM & Ed; Politique Mag; Asian Youth for Civic Engagement; Husky Howler Manage, edit, & write for 2 int'l., 2 nat., & 1 local publications. Direct global teams of writers, publish op-eds, & teach HS journalism class.
Cultural	President, VP (Spring 2020), Sec. (Fall 2019); Middle Georgia State University International Students and Studies Association Guest speaker at 2021 GA Int'l Leadership Conference. Coordinated seven cultural workshops to educate, strengthen, & embrace our diverse student body.
Academic	President, Middle Georgia State University Honors Student Association Host and coordinate the 2021 Georgia Collegiate Honors Council Conference for undergraduates and faculty all over the Southeastern United States.

(continued)

(continued)

Activity	Description
Student Govt./Politics	Student Body President, Junior; Sophomore, Pres.; High School Student Council From planning Homecoming to taking Crazy Hair Day a little too seriously, I'm here for our student body. Forget the fancy title. I'm here to serve.
Debate/Speech	President, Secretary-General, High School Model United Nations (Outstanding & Distinguished Delegation 2020 Valdosta State) Best Delegate (2019 Valdosta). Revived a discontinued club into Howard's 3rd largest organization & hone students' negotiation skills for world peace.
Debate/Speech	Prosecution Attorney, "The Playmaker"; High School Mock Trial Team (3rd in Region 2019); Individual: Best Attorney in Region (2019) I polish my team's direct & cross-examination questions to best convince the jury that the Lyft driver was in fact the mastermind behind the robbery.

(continued)

Activity	Description
Student Govt./Politics	Alumna Advisor; "Last (Wo)man Standing"; Activist, Macon Youth Commission: GA Civics Awareness Program 2019 Grad; Chisholm Leaders; Warren for Pres. Revived local civic participation when advisers abandoned the program in 2019. Speak at nat. conferences. Volunteer presidential & mayoral campaigns.
Religious	Simultaneous Sermon Interpreter Korean to English, Macon Korean Baptist Church Deliver the Lord's message—matching my father not just in diction but also intonation and nuance. Even if it's for one listener, I give it my all.
Work (Paid)	Mathematic Instructor; High School Tutor (Unpaid); Mathnasium of Macon (80+ students); AP Calc; Struggling Freshmen in Foundations/Alg. I (68 students) Nothing compares to witnessing a student's aha moment & improvement. Educating isn't just a job; it's my calling—whether it's with math or my pen.

(continued)

(*continued*)

Activity	Description
Work (Paid)	Marketing Student Assistant, Middle Georgia State University Center for Career and Leadership Development After I redesigned CCLD's marketing strategies, hand-shake activations grew from 700 to 3,000. Getting a job is easy when students use our services!

How This Student Used the *ACCEPTED!* Strategy

Class Spam. Class spam, baby. Next time someone tries to tell you not to worry about how many subjects you take because colleges aren't as interested in this dynamic. Think again. This student did 15 AP exams over four years. She started with simple human geography in Grade 9 nailing a 5. This gave her confidence and momentum to take three in Grade 10. She amped up the intensity and took Calculus AB, Environmental Science, and World History. As her AP test-taking skills continued to improve, she dialed up the intensity one step further in Grade 11 and took five: Calculus BC, US History, Government & Politics, English Language & Composition, and Biology. By Grade 12, she had hit her Super Saiyan stride and took six APs: Statistics, English Literature, Macroeconomics, Microeconomics, Chemistry, and Physics C Mechanics. I emphasized that class spam's associated stress can be dramatically reduced by starting early and spacing out your subjects over many years. This is a fantastic example of this approach in action and the results speak for themselves.

(continued)

Throwing Age and Time Out of the Window.
This student dominated the niche of student journalism. Many ambitious students (myself included) might be the editor of a single student newspaper. This student managed, edited, and wrote for two international, two national, and one local publication. She led a global team of student writers and even taught a high school journalism class. You read that right. She taught a high school journalism class. How hard is all of this to do in reality? Difficult, but not impossible. You can recruit a bunch of student writers. You can read far beyond your age in terms of the media industry and keep practicing your writing skills (which is often a function of how many essays you write and how much feedback you get). This student ran hard and in the same way Procter & Gamble has a portfolio of shampoo brands, she has a portfolio of student publications!

Institutional Leadership Domination with Some Personality. She was student body president. Being the head of her entire high school shows she has great peer support, respect, and teacher endorsement. This adds serious credibility to her whole application and suggests a leadership prowess far beyond her age. Not everyone can be the student body president but if you can aspire for this and get it, it is one epic achievement. Her hilarious personality was shown by her quirky description "From planning Homecoming to taking Crazy Hair Day a little too seriously, I'm here for our student body. Forget the fancy title. I'm here to serve." This student is not a super nerd. She also takes Crazy Hair Day seriously—how can you not love that?

Deep Commitment to Religious Community through Unique Activity. This student was a

(continued)

(*continued*)

"Simultaneous Sermon Interpreter Korean to English, Macon Korean Baptist Church." She describes her activity in a powerful, vivid way that makes you immediately understand how seriously she takes her responsibility and her passionate faith in a matter of words. "Deliver the Lord's message—matching my father not just in diction but also in intonation and nuance. Even if it's for one listener—I give it my all." Her description of matching her father's presentation so carefully shows masterful fluency in both Korean and English. The reference to "the Lord" immediately tells you about her serious faith and how meaningful this is to her identity (especially given her father's direct involvement in the church). I can guarantee Harvard didn't see many simultaneous Korean to English translators applying this year! This is a wonderful, authentic activity.

One More Thing. This student applied from a low-income background and qualified for a fee waiver for her common application. She grew up in a very humble environment. She had a million reasons why she couldn't pull this off (and they would have been valid and reasonable) but she took the cards she was dealt and threw everything she had at this. Truly inspiring stuff.

Case Study 2 The Cricket Playing Class Spammer Destined for Leadership

This student was admitted into Harvard, Brown, Columbia, and Dartmouth.

He recently graduated from Harvard.

Here is a summary of his Common App profile:

Academics

Curriculum and Details	Score
SAT	1550
SAT Subject Tests: (NB: Subject Tests were removed by College Board in 2021)	
Math	800
Chemistry	800
Physics	800
A Levels Self-studied six A Levels on top of the national curriculum:	
Math	A*
Economics	A*
Business Studies	A*
Thinking Skills	A*
Physics	A*
English Language	A*

(continued)

(continued)

Curriculum and Details	Score
NZQA Scholarship Awards (the national scholarship exams for New Zealand):	
Premier Scholar	Top 10 in country
Physics	Outstanding
Geography	Outstanding
History	Outstanding
English	Outstanding
Media Studies	Outstanding
Classical Studies	Outstanding
Statistics	Scholarship
Economics	Scholarship
Agriculture/Horticulture	Scholarship
Art History	Scholarship Pass in 2014
Physical Education	Scholarship Pass in 2014
Economic	Scholarship Pass in 2014
Media Studies	Scholarship Pass in 2014
Geography	Scholarship Pass in 2014
History	Scholarship Pass in 2014
English	Scholarship Pass in 2014

(continued)

Awards

Curriculum/Details	Award
A Levels	
IGCSE Geography	Top In the World
IGCSE Economics	Top in New Zealand
Best Performance over five IGCSE subjects	Top in New Zealand
AS Mathematics	Top Equal In New Zealand
AS Business Studies	Top In The World
AS General Paper	Top In The World
A Level	Top in New Zealand
English Language	Top In The World

Activities/Extracurriculars

Activity	Description
Head Boy	Head student of high school
Cricket	Represented state-level in U19 age group, represented city at U19 and U16, school 1st XI, all five years of high school and earlier. Selected as net bowler for cricket world cup, providing practice to international teams like South Africa, India, West Indies, etc.
Debating	Represented state at school's debating nationals in 2015 as 1st speaker + leader's reply, member of top team in school. Did debating all five years. Adjudicated junior debates.

(continued)

(continued)

Activity	Description
Table Tennis	Represented the state at table tennis nationals three times. Best result was top eight in U18 singles event at nationals. Played all five years of high school competitively.
Model UN	Represented the country at HMUN/YMUN, participated in NZMUN twice. Did model UN for the last two years of high school.
Organized Regional Youth Leaders Forum (Leadership Project)	Organized conference designed for school leaders (head and deputy prefects) from across the region to discuss strategies to combat prevalent student issues related to mental health management, career misinformation, diversity, & inclusion. First time such an event was conducted in the region.
Barbershop Chorus	Sang in the school barbershop chorus, earned top 10 place in national competition. Awarded best music group in school.
Space Camp— Huntsville Alabama	Selected in NZ delegation to the camp. Competitive process organized by Royal Society of New Zealand Science
Volunteer	City's table tennis center. Helped run training events, local competitions, logistics, etc.

(continued)

How This Student Used the *ACCEPTED!* Strategy

Class Spam. This student took six additional A Levels (the equivalent of about 12 AP subjects) outside of school on top of his national curriculum. He was the first ever in his school to do something like this. He focused on quality first then quantity and achieved the highest grade of A* as well as a number of Top in Country and Top in World awards. When most people typically took the national competitive exams NZQA in the last year of university, he broke the norms and took them a year earlier.

Additionally, he took a number of subjects he had never studied before formally such as history, classics, media studies, and agriculture. He identified a number of core competencies to succeed in these exams through structured, argumentative writing and realized that he could cross-apply his talents from English literature and language to this and accumulate more NZQA scholarships. This strategy ultimately led him to place top 10 in the country (effectively top two when factoring in his actual results) as well as winning Dux (Valedictorian) of his school.

Institutional and Entrepreneurial Leadership Roles. The student achieved the holy grail of high school leadership: head boy. This can be called "head of the student government" or many other names, but the point is clear—he had the highest possible leadership role available in the school. This is like magic fireworks for many Ivy League admissions officers. To help complement this, he also started his own regional youth leaders forum showcasing he can ideate, launch, and manage his own projects as well.

(continued)

(continued)

Application of the Results/Effort Ratio. The student was top 10 in the national barbershop quartet. This is competitive and challenging but it is much less difficult than winning a national violin or piano competition. He chose an extracurricular he was passionate about but also had the potential to win at a national level, earning a powerful honor for his application along the way.

Avoiding "Pay to Play" summer programs. Rather than applying for summer programs that admit everyone and have no signaling value, he applied and won funding to attend the competitive Space Camp in Alabama through support of a local science charity. This shows admissions officers that the applicant was highly competitive within the local STEM environment.

Case Study 3 Playing UChicago's Game

This US student was admitted into University of Chicago through the Early Decision 2 Round.

Here is a summary of her Common App profile:

Academics

Curriculum and Details	Score
SAT	1550
SAT Subject Tests: (NB: Subject Tests were removed by College Board in 2021)	
Math Level 2	800
Chemistry	800
AP Subject Tests:	
Computer Science A	5
Calculus BC	5
Chemistry	5
Physics C Mechanics	5
Psychology	4
Biology	
Statistics	
Economics: Macroeconomics	
Economics: Microeconomics	

(continued)

(continued)

Activities/Extracurriculars

Activity	Description
Internship	Microbio Research Intern, CHN Academy of Sciences Conducted experiments on the production of plant-derived chemo-preventive precursor glucoraphanin; used gene knockout and recombination techniques
Other Club/Activity	Cofounder & President, Transfer Student Club Founded club; mentored over 15 students in acclimating to new school; spearheaded creation of FAQ page, guide-book, and blog for students to share stories
Science/Math	Captain, Math Team Captained team of 15 in multiple regional contests; recruited five new members; developed advanced training materials; top individual scorer
Science/Math	Member, Science Olympiad Team 1st place Bedford HS Annual Women in Science Comp.; led team for monthly competitions; led experiments for optics lab event; constructed study guides

(continued)

Activity	Description
Community Service/Volunteer	Member, National Honors Society Passed selective admission; attended regular meetings; performed 20 hrs of community service per year; organized school events such as Seminar Day
Science/Math	Student, Stanford Pre-Collegiate Summer Institutes top performer in discrete math course; excelled in college-level coursework in cryptography, programming, algorithms, number and graph theory
Music/Instrumental	Violinist Played violin and attended weekly lessons since age 10; performed in school orchestra
Computer/Technology	Member, Robotics Team Self-taught C language and programmed robot; constructed robot; performed tests; competed in regional botball competition
Community Service (Volunteer)	Member, Key Club Attended weekly meetings; performed 30 hrs of community service per year; helped events such as town musical, lunch for the homeless, and book sale

(continued)

(*continued*)

Activity	Description
Work (Paid)	Private Tutor Tutored 7 yr old in Chinese; taught basic reading, listening, speaking, and writing; devised lesson plans and homework; shared cultural activities

Highlights of the *ACCEPTED!* Strategy

UChicago ED2. As we discussed, University of Chicago is obsessed with its yield rates and uses two rounds of optional binding admission to assess what students are sincere about wanting to commit to them. This student made the tough decision to commit to UChicago through the binding round (in regular admissions) after trying a more aggressive approach in the early round to some reach schools to solidify her odds of locking in the school. It was a success!

Use of Achievements during Summer to Differentiate. The candidate attended Stanford's Pre-collegiate Summer Institute. This is generally non-selective and so doesn't necessarily signal the student has jumped through any particular hoops. To offset this, the student took her program very seriously and ended up being the highest perform-ing student in the discrete mathematics course. This is a great way to show the student's motivation and talent by thriving in a fairly motivated group of students.

Use of Entrepreneurial Leadership Roles. The student lacked any formal institutional leadership roles within her school's student government so she prioritized a range of her own initiatives to strengthen this part of the profile. She captained her

(continued)

mathematics team (volunteered to serve as captain). She was able to show her impact by highlighting the team's participation in multiple activities, growing the size of the group (albeit modestly) and developing training material. She also created a transfer student club to help new students joining the school with their acclimatization following her own experience.

Case Study 4 Violin, Vaults, and Volunteering—The Triple Flip into the Ivy League

This student was admitted into Dartmouth, UCLA, Tufts, UMichigan, Northeastern, and more.

Here is a copy of his Common App profile:

Curriculum and Details	Score
SAT	1520
SAT Subject Tests: (NB: Subject Tests were removed by College Board in 2021)	
US History	720
Spanish Reading	720
AP Subject Tests:	
US History	4
Spanish Language	5
Psychology	5
Economics: Macroeconomics	5
Economics: Microeconomics	5
Biology	
English Language & Composition	
Environmental Science	
Computer Science Principles	

(continued)

(continued)

Activities/Extracurriculars

Activity	Description
Community Service (Volunteer)	President, Best Buddies International (WY Chapter) Spearheaded music therapy initiative; raised $3,000 for therapy for students w/ disabilities; facilitated and developed 100+ mentor-buddy relationships
Music: Instrumental	Violinist, Chicago Youth Symphony Orchestra Selected through rigorous audition process; prestigious Chicagoland youth orchestra; 14+ free community concerts for public schools; weekly rehearsals
School Spirit	President, WY Freshmen Mentors Organized annual freshman orientation (500+ new students) and BBQ; coordinated team-building activities; paired new students to peer advisors
Athletics: Club	Gymnastics, Captain, IK Gymnastics Chicago Ranked Top 50 '16 '17 USA Gymnastics Men's Trampoline; led practices of 15+ athletes; coordinated team travel and timetables at competitions
Community Service (Volunteer)	ESL Tutor, Heartland Alliance Human Care Taught advanced ESL to adult learners; weekly classes; only high school aged volunteer; 100+ hours of tutoring

(continued)

Activity	Description
Community Service (Volunteer)	President, NJHS (WY Chapter) Coordinated service opportunities for 200+ students at school and in local community; fundraised over $2,000 for Chicagoland charities
Community Service (Volunteer)	Junior Exec. Board Officer, Misericordia Home Social media chair for springtime fundraiser; 150+ hours of service; organized teen outreach camp for prospective residents
Work (Paid)	Gymnastics Coach, IK Gymnastics Progressed from assistant coach to coaching own recreational classes; part-time job
Academic	Student, Yale Young Global Scholars Studied frontiers of science and technology; advanced topics in gene editing and public health; final group presentation on food insecurity
Athletics: JV/Varsity	Sailing, Founding Member, WY Varsity Sailing Team 1 of 15 initial team members; organized transportation to practice on Lake Michigan; fundraised gear and start-up costs

(continued)

(continued)

Awards and Achievements

Details
Dartmouth Book Award (Academic and extracurricular excellence)
State/Regional 11 CIEE Global Navigator Scholarship (Academic achievement)
National Honor Society
Spanish National Honor Society (Sociedad Honoraria Hispánica)
Illinois State Seal of Biliteracy (awarded for proficiency in both English and Spanish)

Highlights of the *ACCEPTED!* Strategy

Domination of a Niche. This student didn't choose to compete in US football or basketball but instead focused on gymnastics. Gymnastics is, of course, a competitive sport, but it is far less popular by student numbers than some of the larger ones. The student was able to rank in the top 50 of US men's gymnastics for two years. Beyond merely competing, he also showed his leadership potential by planning travel schedules and competitions. He built on his passion for gymnastics by doing recreational coaching.

Competitive Summer Programs. The student applied and was admitted into Yale Young Global Scholars. This is a well-recognized program that has some signaling value to US universities. The student also used the program to build on core academic themes such as gene editing, public health, and then he created a project in food security. These are naturally very difficult to pursue in a traditional high school environment and so this demonstrated the students' intellectual vitality.

(continued)

Creating Leadership Opportunities. The student launched his own varsity sailing team and recruited 15 members. Building on the theme of his logistics and operations skill, he arranged the travel schedule to practices on Lake Michigan and oversaw the necessary fundraising to bring the club to life. From these multiple examples across the application, an admissions officer is confident that this student is quite adept at building and growing a community—a very powerful skill on a college campus (and in life!).

Swimming in the Shark Lane. Typically, violin is a competitive bloodbath. However, if you can compete in a competitive swim lane, power to you. This student was able to be selected for the Chicago Youth Symphony Orchestra, which is one of the most prestigious opportunities within his state. Additionally, he continues to show the theme of his logistics and operations skill by supporting to run 14 free community concerts, which is really a huge time commitment. This is good evidence of real depth in one of his main musical activities.

Case Study 5 The Student Athlete Who Competed with Her Head

This student was admitted into Princeton, Stanford, the University of Pennsylvania, and Dartmouth.

Here is a copy of her Common App profile:

Curriculum and Details	Score
SAT	1560

SAT Subject Tests:
(NB: Subject Tests were removed by College Board in 2021)
    Literature
    Math I
	
	780
	780

Higher School Certificate (HSC Australian Curriculum)
ATAR: 99.6
 	
Subjects:
    Mathematics
    Mathematics extension
    English Advanced
    English Extension
    French
    German
    Physics
	99.6 (99.95 being the highest possible score)
	
	99/100 (2nd in year)
	48/50 (4th in year)
	95/100 (2nd in year)
	47/50 (1st in year)
	95/100 (4th in year)
	95/100 (2nd in year)
	91/100 (5th in year)

(continued)

Activities/Extracurriculars

Activity	Description
Athletics: Club	Swim, National Swimmer 2017 Australian Bronze medalist 5k Open Water; Multiple NSW State Gold, Silver, and Bronze medals; 2017 School Swimming Captain.
Academic	2016 Yale Young Global Scholar Attended Yale Young Global Scholars program in Politics, Law and Economics in June 2016. Received award for capstone project on politics and media.
Community Service (Volunteer)	School of St Jude, Tanzania Speaker, fundraiser; member of St Jude's community since age 10 when I first sponsored a student. Involved my school/swim community to fund vaccinations and soccer nets.
Community Service (Volunteer)	VACTERL Group for Kids youth spokesperson I speak at conferences for VGK to reassure parents that their newborns with this association will lead full, happy lives.

(continued)

(continued)

Activity	Description
Internship	Time4Good Intern The brainchild of Yale academic Peter Boyd, my YYGS experience saw me receive this internship where I connected charities with business leaders.
Debate/Speech	Independent Schools Debating Association Debater Represented school in the ISDA Debating Competition for 10 years. Reached semifinals and finals almost every year. First speaker specialist.
Academic	Johns Hopkins Center for Talented Youth Member since age 10. Able to engage in various CTY programs, challenges, classes. Participated in maths, science, and English enrichment programs.
Athletics: JV/Varsity	Cross-country, School/State Cross-Country Representative Represented my school at inter-school cross-country competitions for eight years. Highlight was a silver medal at All-Schools State competition in 2014.
School Spirit	Peer Tutoring As a volunteer tutor in all subjects for girls in younger years, I have loved watching my young friends improve in grades and confidence.

(continued)

Activity	Description
Journalism/ Publication	Writer, School Magazine I have written numerous articles for my student-run school magazine, most notably a story on the positive relationship between academics and sport.

Awards and Achievements

Details
Winner Australian Defense Force Long Tan Leadership Award.
Australian Council Educational Research Language Competition—High Distinction in French and German
Australian Mathematics Competition—High Distinction
Academic Honors—Top 5 in Year overall and first in course for 1+ subjects every year in high school.

Highlights of the ACCEPTED! Strategy

Athletes Competing With Your Head. Despite her intense commitment to her athletics, the student achieved a 1560 in the SAT. This places her above the average accepted score of applicants to schools like Princeton. As sports coaches assess her, they see that she is not only able to contribute on the sporting field but her strong academics enables them to potentially admit other less able athletic students. She becomes an absolute gem for the athletics coaches of the Ivy League schools.

(continued)

(continued)

Avoiding "Pay to Play" summer programs. Yale Young Global Scholars was pursued in the areas of politics, law, and economics. YYGS is a competitive summer program that is well regarded by admissions officers across the US. By choosing this, the applicant signals she has rigorously challenged herself over the summer.

Choosing a Niche and Dominating It. The student was able to use her talent for languages in French and German to stand out from the crowd. Stanford, in particular, values language skills. She was able to achieve high distinction in her national council's educational research language competition.

Showing Relative Achievement in the School Environment, The student was clear to specify that she was consistent in achieving Top 5 overall in her year group every year and winning at least one subject prize each year. This shows that within the context of her school, she was able to dominate academically in a range of academic pursuits. The top US universities really value students who show relative achievement in class rank and are clearly at the top of their school's academic environment.

As you think about your own candidacy, use the *ACCEPTED!* framework to critically evaluate your own current and potential activities to make sure you are best positioning yourself to gain admission. These are just a handful of examples of the principles in action to give you context as you think about your own profile.

Acknowledgments

The African proverb "it takes a village to raise a child" is powerful. My own educational journey took a huge village of people. Crimson's journey so far has involved literally thousands of people all rowing as hard as they can toward our mission. *ACCEPTED!* is no different.

I want to thank my wonderful Crimson head of marketing and loyal supporter, Kimberly Scott. I like to joke that trying to get a book produced is way harder than raising money from venture capitalists. I gave writing a book a crack back in 2018 and found it very confusing to navigate the different publishers and requirements by myself. I originally met Kim because she hired Crimson to support her daughter, who is now an Ivy League graduate. Her faith in Crimson led her to join us to lead our content marketing efforts. She is an extremely talented writer and helped me by introducing me to her legendary agent Harvey Klinger. She worked hard with me to offer her unique perspective and give me feedback at all kinds of wacky hours of the morning and night. *ACCEPTED!* would not be here without Kim.

A huge thank you to Harvey. Thanks for believing in me and my vision for this book. People have written loads of books on college admissions but for the most part they are quite generic, treading carefully and respectfully around established norms. My goal was to break all the rules and write a book that truly reflects the most powerful strategies I have used in my own life and with my students to best amplify their educational journeys. Harvey saw the need and opportunity for this book and jumped in.

Next, thanks to the team at Jossey-Bass/Wiley. In particular, thanks to Amy Fandrei for believing in me and my learnings and philosophy and seeing the value in bringing it to students and their families all over the world. I have loved working with you and seeing how the book publishing industry works from the inside.

Thank you to John Key. You have been an inspiration to me for many years as a shining example of a Kiwi who crushed tall poppy syndrome, embraced your ambition, and then shared your wisdom with New Zealand to benefit our society. Your journey from New Zealand to Wall Street to leading our country from strength to strength as prime minister for 10 years helped to inspire many Kiwis including myself and Fangzhou to aim higher.

Thank you to the whole Crimson team. Your hard work every day changes the lives and opportunities of thousands of students directly through your services and millions indirectly through your viral online content. Your energy for our mission is addictive and keeps me running as fast as I can to help us get to each new milestone for our students, families, and team.

A special thank you to my executive team including Andrew Wooten, David Freed, and Elizabeth Jurlina. I wouldn't have had the opportunity or the time to write this book if it weren't for your strong management, leadership, and operational excellence in supporting me to grow Crimson.

Thank you to Fangzhou. You are my brother-from-another-mother and helped Crimson unleash its potential on the world stage. You inspire me with your commitment to leveling up and continuing to pursue your education while being a phenomenal leader for Crimson. Your commitment to our students at Crimson is absolute and I know I can count on you as I would my own family.

Thank you to Sharndre, our Crimson cofounder (along with Fangzhou) whose devotion to Crimson for eight years helped me to balance the crazy years at Harvard when we were straddling a growing organization with our undergraduate studies and were on opposite sides of the world.

Thank you to my partner, Nensy. You have been by my side every single day of making this book, supporting me and cheering me on. Your love, encouragement, and belief in me gives me a kind of rocket fuel that never seems to run out.

Thank you to our students and families for trusting me with the most serious moments of your education journey. It may look obvious now but to our early clients who put their faith in me when I was 18, still had my braces on, and had no track record other than my own academics, your faith in how I could help you created a snowball that continues to roll faster and faster, affecting more students.

Thank you to Adriaan Van de Wetering for teaching me how to negotiate and supporting Crimson's early growth into new support areas.

Thank you to my mentors, investors, and supporters who are too numerous to acknowledge individually. In particular, thank you to Julian Robertson for seeing my vision at Crimson and backing me before anyone else did, not only with your capital but also with your mentorship, philosophy, insights, and network. Your support led us to take Crimson from affecting a small pool of Kiwis in Auckland, to being a global leader in university admissions support, changing the lives of young people from all over the world.

Thank you to Janine Manning for being my Crimson mum for many years now and giving your brilliant feedback on the book. You have supported me with complete faith since our earliest days and taught me many of the foundational components of running a company professionally.

Finally, and most important, thank you to my whole family: Glenn, granny and grandad, and my mother, Paula Beaton. Mum, you made me the center of your universe for 18 years and covered me in buckets of love. I get to look a bit knowledgeable and wise these days, but the truth is I owe all my learnings, educational journey, and opportunities to you and your clairvoyance. You had the stamina and vision to ignore the conventional parenting wisdom in New Zealand and raise me in your own distinctive style. You inspired me with your own educational journey, values, and work ethic and cheered me on every day. You sat next to me and trained me for all my exams and studies for many years. You worked hard to invest in my education and give me a set of opportunities many students in our position would not have been able to access. You are the best mum in the world, period.

That's a wrap!

About the Author

Jamie Beaton graduated from Harvard University, magna cum laude in 2016 (two years ahead of schedule) with a double degree in Applied Mathematics-Economics and Applied Math. He was also one of the youngest in the world to be accepted to Stanford's Graduate School of Business at age 20.

In June 2019, Jamie graduated from Stanford with an MBA and MA in Education—the youngest-ever recipient of the Arjay Miller Award (Top 10% of his class). He then began his PhD (DPhil) in Public Policy from Oxford University's Blavatnik School of Government as a Rhodes Scholar.

As cofounder and CEO of Crimson Education, Jamie now helms a company dedicated to leveling the playing field in world-leading university admissions. With more than 400 Ivy League, 2,500 US Top 50, 133 Oxford or Cambridge, and 950+ UK Top 10 university offers under his leadership belt, Jamie continues to mentor students personally from his home in New York City.

Notes

CHAPTER 1: SIGNALING, THE HUNGER GAMES, AND McHARVARD

1. Becker, Gary S. *Human Capital: A Theoretical and Empirical Analysis, with Special Reference to Education.* 2d ed. New York: Columbia University Press for NBER, 1975.
2. Evan Spiegel is the cofounder and CEO of Snap. His estimated worth is $US13 billion. https://www.forbes.com/profile/evan-spiegel/?sh=7b5a3b4f529c
3. Parker, Tim. Where Do Unicorn Founders Go to College? Investopia.com. Updated August 17, 2020. https://www.investopedia.com/articles/small-business/021017/where-do-unicorn-founders-go-college.asp

CHAPTER 2: CLASS SPAM: DEADLY AND EFFECTIVE

1. Guide to AS and A-Level Results for England, 2020. https://www.gov.uk/government/news/guide-to-as-and-a-level-results-for-england-2020
2. Stanford Undergraduate Admission. Selection Process. Updated March 19, 2021. https://admission.stanford.edu/apply/selection/

3. Lee, Kai-Fu. *AI Superpowers: China, Silicon Valley, and the New World Order.* Boston: Houghton Mifflin, 2018.

4. Levitt, Steven D., and Stephen J. Dubner. *Freakonomics: A Rogue Economist Explores the Hidden Side of Everything.* New York: Harper Perennial, 2009.

5. Jaschik, Scott. Inside Education. Rejecting AP Courses. June 19, 2018. https://www.insidehighered.com/news/2018/06/19/eight-private-high-schools-washington-area-are-dropping-out-ap-program

6. International Baccalaureate. 2021. https://www.ibo.org/

CHAPTER 3: EARLY DECISION AND THE DATING GAME

1. Yahoo! Finance. *U.S. News & World Report* Announces Strategic Relationship with Crimson Education. August 17, 2020. https://finance.yahoo.com/news/u--news-world-report-announces-040100802.html

2. University of Chicago Admissions. First Year Application Plans, 2021. https://collegeadmissions.uchicago.edu/apply/first-year-applicants/first-year-application-plans

3. University of Chicago Nobel Laureates. 2020. https://www.uchicago.edu/about/accolades/nobel_laureates/

4. University of Chicago Class of 2024 Profile. https://collegeadmissions.uchicago.edu/apply/class-2024-profile

5. *U.S. News & World Report.* 2021 Best National University Rankings. https://www.usnews.com/best-colleges/rankings/national-universities

CHAPTER 4: MORPHEUS WINS: "SHOW ME THE FUTURE!"

1. Stanford University Facts. Other Undergraduate Education Facts. Top Undergraduate Majors By Enrollment 2019–2020. https://facts.stanford.edu/academics/undergraduate-facts/
2. Caldera, Camille G. Economics Remains Most Popular Concentration for Class of 2022. *The Harvard Crimson*. December 13, 2019. https://www.thecrimson.com/article/2019/12/13/concentration-numbers-2019/
3. Harvard University College Handbook for Students. Fields of Concentration. Folklore and Mythology. 2021. https://handbook.fas.harvard.edu/book/folklore-and-mythology

CHAPTER 5: THE EXTRACURRICULAR RESULTS/EFFORT RATIO: WHAT IT IS, HOW IT WORKS, AND WHY IT MATTERS

1. Trinity College London. Music Diplomas. Performance Diplomas. https://www.trinitycollege.com/qualifications/music/diplomas/performance
2. Trinity College London. Speech and Drama Diplomas. https://www.trinitycollege.com/qualifications/drama/diploma-exams
3. MIT RSI. Center for Excellence in Education. Research Science Institute. 2021. https://www.cee.org/programs/research-science-institute

CHAPTER 6: NOT A SCHOOL LEADER? GO BUILD YOUR OWN EMPIRE

1. Harvard University, CS50: Introduction to Computer Science. 2021. https://online-learning.harvard.edu/course/cs50-introduction-computer-science?delta=0
2. Coursera offered by Stanford Online. Machine Learning. Instructor Andrew Ng. 2021. https://www.coursera.org/learn/machine-learning
3. Lee, Kai-Fu. *AI Superpowers: China, Silicon Valley, and the New World Order*. Boston: Houghton Mifflin, 2018.

CHAPTER 7: DON'T BE FOOLED: RECOMMENDATION LETTERS ARE AUDIT TRAILS

1. Duke of Edinburgh Award. https://www.dofe.org/do/what/
2. Eton College UK. Official website 2021. https://www.etoncollege.com/
3. Phillips Academy Andover. About Us. History. 2021. https://www.andover.edu/about/history

CHAPTER 8: THE KINGMAKERS: HERE'S HOW THE BEST OF THE BEST DEFEAT THE REST OF THE BEST OF THE BEST

1. International Mathematical Olympiad (IMO). 2021. http://www.imo-official.org/
2. International Biology Olympiad (IBO). 2021. https://www.ibo-info.org/en/

3. International Chemistry Olympiad (IChO). 2021. https://www.ichosc.org/

4. International Young Physics Tournament. 2021. https://www.iypt.org/

5. MIT RSI. Center for Excellence in Education. Research Science Institute. 2021. https://www.cee.org/programs/research-science-institute

6. MIT RSI statistics. After Center for Excellence Education (CEE): College/University. 2021 https://www.cee.org/about-us/after-cee-collegeuniversity

7. Regeneron International Science and Engineering Fair. 2021. https://www.societyforscience.org/isef/

CHAPTER 9: IT'S ALL OPTIONAL!— WHAT THE NEW "TEST OPTIONAL" UNIVERSE MEANS TO COLLEGE ADMISSIONS

1. *U.S. News & World Report*. Harvard University. Overview. Average SAT scores. https://www.usnews.com/best-colleges/harvard-university-2155

2. SunLive Media. Mount Teen Takes It to Harvard. December 28, 2019. https://www.sunlive.co.nz/news/230444-mount-teen-takes-it-to-harvard.html

3. Lu, Vivi E., and Dekyi T. Tsotsong, Harvard College Receives Record-High 57,000 Applications, Delays Admissions Release Date. *The Harvard Crimson*. January 22, 2021. https://www.thecrimson.com/article/2021/1/22/harvard-class-of-2025-applications-record-high/

4. Wen, Anne. Princeton Postpones Admissions Decision Date. *The Daily Princetonian*. January 31, 2021. https://www.dailyprincetonian.com/article/2021/02/princeton-ivy-league-undergraduate-admissions-date-postponed

5. College Board Blog. January 19, 2021. College Board Will No Longer Offer SAT Subject Tests or SAT with Essay. https://blog.collegeboard.org/January-2021-sat-subject-test-and-essay-faq

6. Bousselaire, Sloan. The Borgen Project. Hagwon Schools in South Korea. October 25, 2017. https://borgenproject.org/hagwons-south-korea/

CHAPTER 10: POWERADE, BURGER PATTIES, AND THE PERFECT PERSONAL STATEMENT

1. Crimson Education. Te Ara a Kupe Beaton Scholarship. 2021. https://www.crimsoneducation.org/au/about-us/te-ara-a-kupe-beaton-scholarship/

CHAPTER 11: DUAL DEGREES AND WHY DOUBLE DIPPING OPENS DOORS YOU MAY NOT KNOW EXISTED

1. Glaeser, Edward. *Triumph of the City*. New York: Pan Books, 2012.

2. The University of Pennsylvania. The Huntsman Program in International Studies and Business. 2021. https://huntsman.upenn.edu/

3. The University of Pennsylvania. Engineering at Wharton. The Jerome Fisher Program in Management and Technology. 2021. https://fisher.wharton.upenn.edu/

4. Brown University/Rhode Island School of Design (RISD) Dual Degree Program. 2021. https://www.brown.edu/academics/brown-risd-dual-degree/

5. The University of California Berkeley Management, Entrepreneurship and Technology (MET) Program. 2021. https://met.berkeley.edu/

6. Harvard University. Dual Degree Music Programs. Harvard New England Conservatory. 2021. https://college.harvard.edu/academics/liberal-arts-sciences/dual-degree-music-programs

7. Columbia University Undergraduate Admissions. Columbia-Juilliard Program. 2021. https://undergrad.admissions.columbia.edu/apply/first-year/juilliard-program

8. Stanford University. Coterminal Master's Degrees. https://exploredegrees.stanford.edu/cotermdegrees/

9. Columbia University. Combined Plan Program Experience. 3-2 Sequence. 2021. https://undergrad.admissions.columbia.edu/learn/academiclife/engineering/combined-plan-program

10. University of Pennsylvania. Roy and Diana Vagelos Program in Life Sciences & Management. School of Arts and Sciences. Wharton. 2021. https://lsm.upenn.edu/

11. University of Pennsylvania. Digital Media Design Program. 2021. http://cg.cis.upenn.edu/dmd.html

CHAPTER 12: WHAT THE RICH GET WRONG: DON'T PAY TO PLAY OVER SUMMER

1. Harvard Summer School. Summer Programs for High School Students. 2021. https://summer.harvard.edu/high-school-programs/

2. Stanford University. Stanford University Mathematics Camp. (SUMaC). 2021. https://sumac.spcs.stanford.edu/

3. Yale University. Yale Young Global Scholars program (YYGS). 2021. https://globalscholars.yale.edu/

4. The Summer Science Program. 2021. https://summer-science.org/

CHAPTER 13: WHY STUDENT ATHLETES NEED TO COMPETE WITH THEIR HEADS

1. Harvard University Athletics. https://gocrimson.com/

2. Wang, William L. Filings Show Athletes with High Academic Scores Have 83 Percent Acceptance Rate. *The Harvard Crimson*. June 30, 2018. https://www.thecrimson.com/article/2018/6/30/athlete-admissions/

CHAPTER 14: MANAGING YOUR TOUGHEST ADVERSARY—YOUR MIND!

1. Lu, Vivi E., and Dekyi T. Tsotsong. Harvard College Accepts Record-Low 3.43% of Applicants to Class of 2025. *The Harvard Crimson*. April 2021. https://www.thecrimson.com/article/2021/4/7/harvard-admissions-2025/

CHAPTER 15: INTERNATIONAL STUDENTS AND THE EVEN MORE UNEVEN PLAYING FIELD

1. Worldometer. World Population 2020. United States Population. https://www.worldometers.info/world-population/us-population/

2. Harvard University. Harvard Class of 2025 Profile. https://college.harvard.edu/admissions/admissions-statistics

3. EducationData.org. International Student Enrollment Statistics. February 20, 2021. https://educationdata.org/international-student-enrollment-statistics

4. *U.S. News & World Report.* 2021 Best Global Universities Rankings. 2021. https://www.usnews.com/education/best-global-universities/rankings

5. MIT Admissions. Class of 2024. https://mitadmissions.org/apply/process/stats/

6. MIT Admissions. Class of 2023. https://web.archive.org/web/20190817142743/https://mitadmissions.org/apply/process/stats/

7. MIT Admissions. Class of 2020. https://web.archive.org/web/20170723124341/https://mitadmissions.org/apply/process/stats/

8. University of Pennsylvania. Facts. Class of 2024. https://www.upenn.edu/about/facts

9. University of Pennsylvania. Facts. Class of 2022. https://web.archive.org/web/20190816131720/https://www.upenn.edu/about/facts

10. University of Pennsylvania. Facts. Class of 2019. https://web.archive.org/web/20160529194037/http://www.upenn.edu/about/facts

11. Princeton University. Profile Class of 2022. https://pr.princeton.edu/pub/profile/PU Profile 201819.pdf

12. Princeton University. Profile Class of 2010. https://pr.princeton.edu/profile/06/08.htm

13. Princeton University. Profile Class of 2005. https://pr.princeton.edu/profile/01/08.htm

14. Princeton University. Profile Class of 2000. https://pr.princeton.edu/profile/96/08.html

15. University of California Berkeley. Class of 2023. International Student Data. https://admissions.berkeley.edu/international-students

16. University of California Berkeley. Class of 2022. Admissions Data. https://web.archive.org/web/20190729171525/https://admissions.berkeley.edu/student-profile

17. University of California Berkeley. Class of 2021. Admissions Data. https://web.archive.org/web/20180626193557/https://admissions.berkeley.edu/student-profile

18. University of California Berkeley. Class of 2023. International Student Data. https://admissions.berkeley.edu/international-students

19. University of California Berkeley. Class of 2023. Admissions Data. https://admissions.berkeley.edu/student-profile

20. University of California Berkeley. Class of 2023. International Student Data. https://admissions.berkeley.edu/international-students

21. University of California Berkeley. Class of 2023. Admissions Data. https://admissions.berkeley.edu/student-profile

CHAPTER 16: MONEYBALL—HOW TO RANK AND CHOOSE THE BEST UNIVERSITIES

1. Sheinerman, Marie-Rose. U. Ranked No. 1 American University by *U.S. News* for 10th Consecutive Year. *The Daily Princetonian*. September 14, 2020. https://www.dailyprincetonian.com/article/2020/09/princeton-top-university-in-america-us-news-report-10-years

2. Moody, Josh. Universities, Colleges Where Students Are Eager to Enroll. *U.S. News & World Report.* January 25, 2021. https://www.usnews.com/education/best-colleges/articles/universities-colleges-where-students-are-eager-to-enroll

3. This data is estimated/reported by various sources including Parchment.com. https://www.parchment.com/c/college/tools/college-cross-admit-comparison.php?compare=Harvard+University&with=Stanford+University

4. *U.S. News & World Report.* 2021 Best National University Rankings. https://www.usnews.com/best-colleges/rankings/national-universities

CHAPTER 17: HARVARD'S LEGACY, MY LEGACY, AND YOUR LEGACY

1. Gross, Daniel A. How Elite US Schools Give Preference to Wealthy and White 'Legacy' Applicants. *The Guardian.* January 23, 2019. https://www.theguardian.com/us-news/2019/jan/23/elite-schools-ivy-league-legacy-admissions-harvard-wealthier-whiter

2. Oxford University Endowment Management estimates endowment value at £4.5 billion in 2020 which is ~equal to $US6.2 billion. https://www.ouem.co.uk/the-oxford-endowment-fund/; Harvard University fy2020 Financial Year Report reports Harvard's end of FY endowment worth to be $US41.9 billion. https://finance.harvard.edu/files/fad/files/fy20_harvard_financial_report.pdf

3. Adams, Susan. Legacy Admissions Banned at Colorado's Public Colleges. *Forbes.* June 1, 2021. https://www.forbes.com/sites/susanadams/2021/06/01/legacy-admissions-banned-at-colorados-public-colleges/?sh=42cc144c573e

CHAPTER 18: THE PERSONALITIES OF THE IVY LEAGUES AND WHICH ONE MAY BE RIGHT FOR YOU

1. Dougan, Patrice. Is Soumil Singh New Zealand's Smartest Teen? *New Zealand Herald*. April 12, 2016. https://www.nzherald.co.nz/nz/is-soumil-singh-new-zealands-smartest-teen/YJX3T4SEN3UJ4GOUWBVP TXWDDY/

Index